COACHING HOCKEY

COACHING HOCKEY

David Whitaker

THE CROWOOD PRESS

First published in 1986 by
THE CROWOOD PRESS
Ramsbury, Marlborough
Wiltshire, SN8 2HE

British Library Cataloguing in Publication Data

Whitaker, David
  Coaching hockey.
  1. Hockey coaching
  I. Title
  796.35′5′077   GV1017.H7
ISBN 0-946284-18-0

Dedicated to Chris, Kester and Alex

Acknowledgements

Figs 183 to 194 by John Hurst,
all other photographs by Morley Pecker

Line illustrations by Vanetta Joffe

Front cover photograph by
John Evans, courtesy of Slazenger Ltd

Typeset by Alacrity Phototypesetters,
Banwell Castle, Weston-super-Mare.
Printed in Great Britain.

Contents

Introduction   1
1 The Coaching Art   5
2 Methods of Play   21
3 Promoting and Developing
   On the Ball Skills   31
4 Promoting and Developing
   Off the Ball Skills   69
5 Attacking Tactics in Open Play   85
6 Defensive Tactics in Open Play   103
7 Tactics at Set Pieces and Restarts   115
8 Coaching for Goalkeepers   133
9 Assessing Teams and Players   141
10 Training for Hockey   147
   Index   152

David Whitaker has coached England since 1980 and Great Britain since 1983. He trained as a PE teacher at Loughborough, and was Head of Physical Education at Marlborough College before his appointment as full time coach to England. In a distinguished playing career, he won 103 caps for England and Great Britain between 1973 and 1980.

I have been lucky enough to have witnessed at close hand David Whitaker's progress from a university player, through a distinguished playing career for England and Great Britain, to the heights achieved as coach to the Great Britain men's hockey team in that memorable bronze medal winning Olympic campaign in Los Angeles in 1984.

Since then, David's stature as a coach and especially as a tactician has continued to grow, and it is fortunate that he has found time to put on paper the thoughts on the art of coaching that have earned him such respect and admiration within the game.

Chris Cox
Chairman, Hockey Association Coaching Committee

This book provides a unique opportunity for schoolteachers and coaches to benefit from the thoughts of one of Great Britain's most experienced players and successful coaches. It is written and illustrated clearly, and offers a wealth of ideas for individual, group and team practices.

Bernard Cotton
Former England and Great Britain Captain Assistant Manager Great Britain

The great players in current international hockey are those who combine their individual flair with sound tactical skills. Without the sound principles outlined in this book, the flair alone would make little or no impact on the well organised teams found in hockey today.

Richard Dodds
Captain of Great Britain

Introduction

This book contains more on tactics, methods of play and group skills, than on the teaching of individual skills. This is a deliberate policy as the teaching of skills is well documented in many other publications, whereas few attempts have been made to assess and describe tactics and group skills. The principal aim of this book, therefore, is to provide for this gap in hockey literature; however, in order to achieve this, some detail relating to hockey skills and the development of these skills is essential.

I have been fortunate over the last sixteen years to have been involved in the playing and coaching of hockey at many levels, participating in over 200 international matches as player or coach on both grass and artificial turf. During this time even the least absorptive brain will collect a considerable amount of knowledge concerning individual and group skills, tactics and team preparation, and it is my hope to document some of this information in such a way as to help both coaches and players.

The skills, tactics and concepts discussed and illustrated in this book are drawn from the international game and, once again, this is deliberate policy, as there is little difference in the factors fundamental to any of these areas between school, club and international hockey. The differences between these levels of hockey lie in the speed, accuracy and consistency of the execution of skills, along with the depth of understanding of tactics and the ability to recognise cues and respond accord-

ingly. The difference between levels of hockey achievement is, therefore, more to do with the ability to respond to increases in environmental stress than the learning of a set of international skills when a player achieves representative hockey. It is my opinion, therefore, that the sooner young players learn skills, both with and without the ball, relevant to the international game, the greater the chance of the better players fulfilling their potential and the healthier our game.

The one factor which at present sets international hockey apart is that it is always played on artificial turf, but I would encourage players and coaches not to concern themselves with worries that the game on artificial turf is vastly different. Differences there are, but the fundamentals of hockey are common to both grass and artificial surfaces and the rapid expansion of the latter will lead to most league and representative hockey being played on this type of pitch.

The ideas and practices put forward are merely part of one man's view and should be seen as a beginning rather than a definitive work. The reader will no doubt agree with some points, question others and improve still more, and that is both healthy and good. If by the end of the book I have assisted the reader in extending his knowledge of group and individual skills, skill learning, tactics, the methods and importance of practising, and team preparation then I shall have achieved my principal aim.

It is almost impossible to acknowledge

1

Fig 1   Great Britain's Jon Potter closing down the Indian forward ...

Fig 2   ... and completing the tackle. (Great Britain v Perth 1985)

all the people who have played a part in this book, for many of them have helped without really knowing it. Bob McLeish began the process in the 1960s at Hitchin Boys Grammar School, after which Loughborough, Blueharts and Southgate all helped enormously by offering me the opportunity to play and cut my teeth in terms of coaching and tactical apprecia- tion. People such as Tony Ekins, Bernie Cotton, Roger Self, Mike Corby, John Cadman and Trevor Clarke have given much appreciated advice during my time as player and coach, all of which has helped formulate the ideas in this book, as have all those left wingers who taught me to defend by beating me so often! For Chapter 8 I am indebted to John Hurst and Ian Taylor.

While acknowledging all these people and others too numerous to mention, I must save my greatest thanks for Chris who, having already put up with fifteen years of hockey, undertook the task of deciphering my writing, putting it into readable English and presenting it in type. On completing the task, she de- clared that it had motivated her to take up sport – squash!

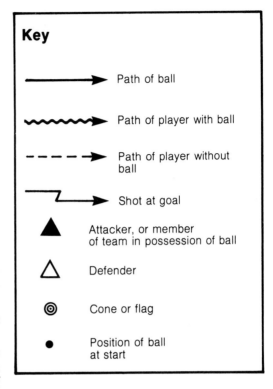

Key	
→	Path of ball
⌇→	Path of player with ball
- - - →	Path of player without ball
⌐→	Shot at goal
▲	Attacker, or member of team in possession of ball
△	Defender
◎	Cone or flag
●	Position of ball at start

Fig 3 'Discretion is the better part of valour.' (India v Australia, 1982)

1 The Coaching Art

Learn something new every day.

However much you think you know, the best coaches (and players) are receptive and perceptive. The former allows them to consider new ideas with an open mind, while the latter illustrates an ability to gain new knowledge from any practice or game situation. Coaches and players who close their eyes and ears never, in my experience, fulfil their potential.

ROLE OF THE COACH

No matter what level, the principal role of the coach is to *co-ordinate the playing resources* at his disposal into the most efficient team possible. The resources for which he has direct responsibility are:

1. Technical – skills; tactics; players' roles; method of play.
2. Physiological – fitness.
3. Psychological – motivation.

However, all coaches have to reconcile these areas of development with the major constraints which impose restrictions upon the 'ideal situation'. These include:

* The facilities available.
* The selection of the players.
* The finance available.
* The time available with the team.
* The time available to individual players for personal training.

It is imperative that the coach evaluates the interaction of these factors and, having given them due consideration, makes realistic expectations of individual and team progress over a given time-scale.

It is admirable to have high expectations but it is foolish to be blind to reality – 'Rome was not built in a day'.

DUTIES OF THE COACH

In pursuit of successfully co-ordinating the playing resources, a coach has to understand and perform a number of functions. These include:

1. Teaching, modifying and sharpening individual skills.
2. Integrating individuals into group skills (team work) and guiding this dovetailing of abilities.
3. Establishing and explaining the team's overall method of play.
4. Formulating and communicating the roles of players within the team.
5. Devising, developing and communicating tactics within the pattern of play.
6. Planning and monitoring the physical preparation of the team.
7. Motivating and maintaining the players' interest.
8. Planning and implementing the practices so that there is progression in both the individual sessions and the overall series of practices.

While the efficient performance of these

duties may provide a blueprint for success, the key attributes common to the best coaches and which work together to change potential into reality are *knowledge* and *communication*.

AREAS OF KNOWLEDGE

Individual and Group Skills

Skills include work both with and without the ball. The former includes amongst others control, passing and shooting, while the latter includes marking, tackling, covering and supporting. The coach must have a detailed knowledge of the skills he is teaching, as this will enable him to:

1. Break down the skill into sections to facilitate learning.
2. Diagnose and rectify faults and weaknesses.
3. Identify key factors that influence the success of the skill.

This is an enormous area of knowledge and the coach has to ask himself a great many questions in order to achieve a detailed understanding of any skill. For example:

* How do the hands and arms move?
* How does the body move?
* Which part moves first?
* Where is the ball positioned?
* Who initiates a move – giver or receiver?
* When does he move?
* What initiates the move?
* When is the pass made?
* Where is the ball passed to?
* What do I do after I have passed the ball?

* What problems can the opposition pose?

Method of Team Play

This relates to the formation upon which the team's pattern of play is to be based. The most widely used are 5-3-2-1; 3-3-3-1-1 and 4-2-3-1-1, although there are variations upon these themes and several other possible formations.

It is important that the coach understands clearly the roles of each position in the formations in both attack and defence and how the various units within the formation function. For example, in the 5-3-2-1, the role of full backs as a unit; full backs plus centre half in defence; centre half plus inside forwards in midfield; inside forward, wing half and wing as a unit; and in the 3-3-3-1-1 the role of sweeper and centre back as a unit; three half backs plus sweeper as a unit; three midfield players as a unit. Only by studying the roles and the requirements for each role can a coach begin to decide on which formation to base a team's play. I say 'base the play' upon a formation, for no two teams play exactly the same, as the strengths and weaknesses of individual players will vary and therefore cause variations in the team play, however slight.

I throw out one interesting fact: of all the leading hockey nations, England and Great Britain have the greatest diversity of playing formation between their national team and the top club, county and divisional sides. In Netherlands, West Germany, India, Pakistan and Australia all the teams immediately below the international level play the same formation. This is not a complaint, merely a statement of fact. It may even be a

Fig 4 Hazelhurst (Australia) looks to exploit space in midfield, while the West German players work hard to get back to mark and cover.

strength of the British game, although I know it does create some difficulties, particularly in developing full backs and inside forwards.

Players' Roles

Which roles are given by the coach to players is, of course, dependent upon matching the requirements of each position in the various formations with the attributes of the players available. It is dangerous to assign particular roles to players who do not possess the required attributes (technical, physical or mental) essential for the successful performance of that role. While it is rare to obtain a perfect fit and therefore quite acceptable to modify a role in accordance with a player's strengths, it is equally important to have a reasonable match between talent and requirement for any particular role. This process can, of course, lead to players playing in a variety of positions. I would actively encourage this, as few are able to find their best playing role early in their hockey career and a knowledge of several positions can enhance not only their individual play, but also their value to a team. The coach should not be afraid of thoughtful experimentation.

Tactics

Every coach must have a knowledge of tactics, but let us not get confused and flustered by the term 'tactics'. An easy definition is 'methods employed to help gain ascendancy over the opposition'.

Tactics can be applied to many situations in the game:

* At an individual level.
* To a group skill level.
* To the team as a whole.
* When your team has possession.
* When the opposition has possession.
* At restarts or in open play.
* In particular areas of the pitch.
* During particular phases of the game.

The skill of the coach is, over a period of time, to make his team or squad tactically aware so that they can then apply the appropriate tactics to a particular game. Tactics cannot be produced out of a hat as if by magic or successfully applied without any prior knowledge on the part of the players. The first part of this coaching skill is completely bound up with the scheme of work planned by the coach and I shall be dealing in detail with this in later chapters, but the ability to choose the appropriate tactics for a particular game needs explanation now.

Tactics ought not to be seen as merely a response to the apparent or supposed strengths of the opposition, as to do this is to negate one's own team play, one of the strongest weapons any team can possess. Likewise, the tactics any team is capable of performing are inextricably bound up with the physical, technical and mental development of the team and its individual players. A coach, therefore, must be sensitive to the tactical capabilities of his players, otherwise he may fall into the trap of asking them to do something of which they are not capable; and then who is to blame when the tactics fail?

Inevitably, the factors which influence the choice of tactics are numerous and interrelated, but can be grouped as follows:

* The overall style of opponents.
* Particular technical, physical or psychological strengths and weaknesses of the opposition.
* Particular tactics/strategies used by the opposition.
* Particular set piece moves used by opponents.
* The development of his own team.
* How the coach anticipates the opposition will react to his team's style of play, strengths, set piece moves, etc.
* The environment: playing surface; heat and humidity; the time elapsed since our/their previous game.
* The type of game to be played. Is it a friendly; practice match; league; cup; etc? How important is the outcome?

All these factors have to be considered by the coach before every game, although the degree of importance given to each aspect may, of course, vary in accordance with changing situations. To perform this tactical role thoroughly and effectively the coach has to have considerable knowledge of his own team and his opposition. This knowledge cannot be gained rapidly and is usually built up over a number of years no matter at what level the coach is working; and the shorter the time available for the preparation of his own team and/or the study of other teams, the more reliance the coach must put on a few key areas.

Having come this far, you may consider this analysis too comprehensive and complex for the day to day games encountered by most of the hockey playing public and their coaches. This may be correct for seventy per cent of club matches, but all successful teams have to win through during a very evenly contested game or tournament and proper preparation by the coach can help swing the odds in the favour of his team. Even more relevant, the higher the standard of competition, the more evenly contested the games and therefore the more impor-

tant the preparation. It is to the coaching of top club teams and representative sides that the factors discussed so far are most applicable.

In any important or evenly contested game, a coach cannot seriously expect his team's pattern of play to dominate throughout, and the best and usually most successful teams are those that cope most successfully during the periods of play in which the opposition dominate. Within a hard-fought match a team may dominate some of the play all of the time (one player may dominate his opponent),

Fig 5   Charlesworth carries the ball through midfield while looking
for support. Notice how the other Australian players
are moving with him. (India v Australia, Karachi 1980)

or all of the play for some of the time, but never can a team dictate all of the play all of the time. The coach must aim to tactically prepare his team so that they not only have every chance of dominating the play for as long as possible, but also are best equipped to cope with the periods of opposition dominance and reduce these to a minimum.

Within any particular game some of the tactics may be implemented at all times, while others only at particular times or positions, whereas some may only be used if certain instances arise (e.g. one goal up or down with five minutes remaining). Probably the most important thing for a coach to remember is that tactics cannot be imposed in spite of the players. For tactics to be successful, players not only have to be capable of performing them but also have to understand and believe in them. To achieve this, communication and trust between players and coach is imperative.

The two fundamental factors in tactical play are *recognition* and *response*; and coaching the tactical aspects of hockey is all about talking through and practising the art of responding correctly to certain cues within the game situation and being able to do so at individual, group and team level. Because the game of hockey is a series of complex interactions, there is rarely only one possible response to a particular cue and, therefore, an integral part of tactical coaching is helping players choose the most effective response, i.e. they must be given the opportunity to be decision makers. It is vital that individuals, groups and the team as a whole are able to 'think on their feet' during the game, and to this end coaches must encourage players to make decisions within the confines of the game plan. The

earlier we help players in this difficult task, the greater the chance of them making the right decisions in the crucial match or in a very pressurised situation in a game.

Physical Requirements

Physiologically hockey is a very demanding game. Not only is aerobic stamina required to complete a match of seventy minutes' duration, but within this structure players perform many sprints of varying intensity and duration, and all these physical demands have to be done with the stick and, at times, while also manipulating the ball.

Part of any coach's role must be to monitor the physical condition of the players and, even if a specialist is used to plan and conduct the physical training, it is important that the coach not only understands the physiological demands of the game but has a working knowledge of the following areas:

1. Aerobic stamina and how to develop it.
2. Anaerobic stamina and how to develop it.
3. Muscular strength and its training.
4. The improvement of a player's speed and acceleration.
5. The importance of mobility (flexibility).

Many teams have access to a Physical Education specialist and they could do no better than to employ his services to construct and implement a simple training programme for the close and early season periods.

The skill element is very important in the game and must, therefore, be included in training as this provides meaning and motivation to many players and whenever possible the coach or trainer should work this into the exercises. Further information and examples of training practices are given in Chapter 10.

Motivating Players

Very few players are able to motivate themselves to such an extent that very little external motivation is necessary. It is, therefore, important that the coach is able to provide the correct stimulus during both the training and competition phase, in order to help each player maximise his performance. Unfortunately, no two players are identical in their psychological make-up and the coach therefore has to vary his approach accordingly. This is quite possible during personal training and discussion sessions, but not so easily done when the whole squad is being coached or a pre-match team talk is being given. In the latter two areas the coach has to find words and phrases best suited to the motivation of the group as a whole, with perhaps occasional modifications aimed at particular individuals.

Before a coach can successfully and consistently motivate a player, he must understand the personality of the player. This knowledge can be gained from questionnaires, but it is also relevant to watch the way he plays and practises and to increase this understanding through discussion. The profile the coach is able to build up using these sources not only provides a great deal of information on which he can base his motivational comments, but also gives him an insight into other important aspects of the player's make-up, for example his attitudes and values; his aspirations; his level of com-

mitment; his personal pressures.

While this aspect may not appear to be very important at club level, it is a vital ingredient of coaching in the international arena and would offer considerable rewards for those coaches and captains of both representative and club sides willing to invest some time in the area. It could enable a team to perform just that little more effectively and, at the crucial times, this is often the difference between success and disappointment.

All methods of motivation, whether in practice or match situations, are variations of the age-old 'stick and carrot' system, although the best coaches have developed innumerable subtleties based on this theme. It is not the aim of this section to teach you how to motivate players, as every coach does this in a unique way, but it may help to lay down some guidelines:

* More demands can be put upon a player in practice sessions.
* Some players need to be told of the relevance of a practice to motivate them to do it properly.
* Players usually respond better to positive rather than negative feedback; for example, comment upon how close the player was to success rather than the fact that he failed.
* Some players practise well but cannot transfer the skill to the game. These need special attention.
* Unfit players hide in the hard practice sessions.
* Even the most committed player gets bored if the practice is too long or is not progressive.
* If a practice requires intensive concentration, then perform it in short sharp spells.

* Sloppy habits in practice lead to sloppy match play.
* Demand high standards from yourself as coach and then you can expect it of the players.

In conclusion, it is important to remember the very first point made in this section: all players will need motivating at some time in practice as well as in match preparation. The art of motivating is providing the necessary comment at the correct moment and delivered in the most effective manner for the individual, group or team. No matter how much knowledge you have, only experience will enable you to get it right more often than not, but the coach with more knowledge has more chance of success!

Age and Expertise of Players

All too often the relationship between players and coach is impaired by the fact that the latter fails to take into account the age and expertise of the players when he is preparing the practice sessions and formulating his expectations and motivational comments. There are characteristics of both young people and less expert players that the coach should appreciate and make allowance for in his coaching.

Young players:

* Are highly enthusiastic, but this can wane rapidly.
* Work in short, sharp bursts of energy.
* Are unable to concentrate on one concept for long periods.
* Are orientated to the individual.
* Gain enjoyment from participation.
* Are less able to cope with failure than adults.

* Are interested in a wide range of activities rather than just hockey.
* Are in the process of developing co-operation with others.
* Are developing the ability to perform fine motor skills and are therefore prone to clumsiness.
* Have difficulty in following complex instructions and focusing their attention on a few important points; all information is given the same priority.
* Require a 'model' of the skill to imitate as they have little or no previous experience to fall back on.
* Have difficulty in recognising when to use a particular skill.

These generalisations will, of course, vary between both groups and individuals with age and experience but they do have important implications for coaching young players. The key elements are simplicity and progression so as to maximise the chances of success at each stage. Here is a possible format:

1. Break a skill down into simple stages so that there is a progression of both skill complexity and information with which the young player is able to cope.
2. Keep the progressions small and do not move on to more complex skills until players are able to cope with them.
3. Structure the progressions so that the young players can learn to recognise the important cues which affect the performance of their skill, for example, when tackling, the position and movement of the ball is the major cue, not any stick or body movement performed by the opponent.
4. Participation and enjoyment are vital if the interest of young players is to be maintained.

Fig 6 Holland drive forward while Great Britain work hard to close the player down and provide cover.

Coaches are often called upon to improve the performance of adult players who suffer from lack of expertise and it is equally important in these circumstances to make allowances in the coaching method.

Experienced players with less expertise may have the following characteristics:

* They do not find it easy to change an ingrained technique or point of view.
* They often dislike practices isolated from the game.
* They are competitive.
* They have the ability to concentrate, but often have little desire to work hard on a particular area for any length of time.
* They are impatient to progress to the more complex skill or game situation.

It will be clear to the reader that here are a different set of characteristics which require an approach that may be similar in some aspects to that advised for young players, but would have to differ in others in order to achieve the desired objectives of any coaching session, i.e. to learn; to enjoy the process; and to instil the desire to learn more.

Plan Progressive and Meaningful Practices

Progressive practices are the means by which a coach efficiently achieves his objectives in any skill or tactical practice, whether it be with a group or an individual. The planning of these practices is one of the least documented areas of coaching and yet it is fundamental to the coaching and learning process.

The aim of practising is to enable players to learn, modify and perfect skills

13

and tactical moves in such a way that they are able to reproduce them in the game situation. Inherent in this aim, therefore, is the fact that the skill or tactic has in the end to be performed under stressful conditions and it is the degree of stress applied to a practice that provides the progression. The degree of stress can be varied in any practice along three pathways:

1. Competitive stress.
2. Skill stress.
3. Spatial stress.

A brief explanation of each will help the reader establish ways in which a coach can use these pathways of increasing stress.

COMPETITIVE STRESS

This ranges between non-competitive and competitive and is altered by increasing or decreasing:

1. The level of opposition inhibiting the successful completion of the activity, for example:

* cones
* passive defender
* active defender (including perhaps some conditions on movement)
* passive defenders
* active defenders (no conditions).

2. The time available in which to perform the activity once or several times (competition against the clock).
3. The amount of time given between each repetition, for example, one, two or multiple ball practices.

It is, of course, possible to combine the three ways of changing competitive stress, so that there is greater sophistication in the progressive practices for any activity along this single pathway.

SKILL STRESS

This quite simply varies from simple skills to complex or more difficult skills. The degree of stress in this area may be increased by the very nature of the skill being learned or practised, for example an aerial flick is intrinsically more difficult than a pushed pass, but it can also be affected by demanding more of the player before, during and/or after the performance of the skill. For example, controlling the ball on the open stick:

1. Stationary.
2. Receiving ball from various directions.
3. Ball is lifted to receiver.
4. Receiver moves (in various directions) before receiving the ball.
5. As above, plus receiver controls the ball and moves on in the same direction.
6. As above, but receiver controls the ball and then changes direction with the ball.
7. Receiver controls the ball and then passes to predetermined points. *Note* this progression can be done with as little or as much preliminary work as the coach desires, for example receive in stationary position and make pass or merely add it to the preceding practice.
8. As above, plus various types of pass or shot at goal.

I am sure the reader can add to this progression.
   Note: in the example above, the degree of competitive and spatial stress has been

kept as constant as possible, but the coach could quite easily develop these simultaneously.

SPATIAL STRESS

This progression is concerned with the space available in which to perform the skill or tactic and obviously develops from an uncongested to a congested situation. The degree of stress is altered by changing the size and/or the shape of the space. It must be noted, however, that it is not always the smallest (or most congested) space that provides the most testing conditions for all skills and tactical practices. Consider the principles of defending, whether as an individual or a group. They are more easily practised in space congested by limited size or the number of defenders occupying it, and this has important ramifications on progressive practices aimed at improving defensive techniques. The reverse is generally true for attacking techniques, i.e. success is more easily attained if the space is large or uncongested.

Through the thoughtful use of these concepts, the coach is able not only to plan accurately a series of progressions that will enable him to achieve predetermined objectives, but also to quickly and easily modify the progressions so that they are at the appropriate level for the player or players.

Having said this, there are two important factors that the coach ignores at his peril. Firstly, a good series of progressions only has one or two major objectives, as it is very difficult for learning and practising to be effective if there are too many objectives. This is especially important when coaching young or less expert players. Secondly, there is a subtle

difference between preparing progressions for practice and teaching. In the latter, the end product is the successful performance of the skill or tactic in its entirety, whereas practising is the performance of the complete skill or tactic under conditions of increasing stress so that it can be reproduced in the game situation. I do not wish to 'split hairs', but it is important to recognise and make allowance for the difference when planning a coaching session. For example, when teaching, it is wise to set the spatial stress at a level that maximises the chance of success, keep the competitive stress to a minimum and make the progressions along the skill pathway.

Learning Process

Clearly, improved performance at any sport is about learning and, therefore, an understanding of the learning process is an important part of the coach's knowledge. The overall aim is to perform the skills and tactics in the game situation, but it is advantageous to isolate them when they are being learnt so that the learning can be done efficiently. A simple skill may be taught in its entirety and progressions used to groove and integrate it into game-like situations. Here the learning is done quickly, and practising rapidly becomes the major objective of any progressions. However, a more complex skill or tactic may itself be broken down into simple progressions to make the learning as easy as possible.

To facilitate the learning process the following well-known pattern is one coaches would do well to emulate in their presentation.

1. *Picture of the skill* A clear illustration

through film or demonstration of the complete skill and a brief explanation of why it is important.

2. *Demonstration* Clear, good quality demonstration along with concise explanation of main points of technique. Remember to keep it simple initially, so allowing players to use 'observation' and 'discovery'.

3. *Trials* Players attempt to perform the skill. An initial trial can be given immediately after the demonstration and before any points of technique are made if the coach considers that the players will benefit from 'feeling' the skill.

4. *Feedback* Information regarding the effectiveness and correctness of performance is vital, but do not make changes to technique unless the errors are inhibiting the performance of the skill.

5. *Modification* Any modifications should be practised and further feedback provided.

Once the skill or tactic has been learnt, practising takes priority in order to integrate it into the game situation. There is no doubt that during this phase of introducing stress more learning takes place in order to successfully perform the skill or tactic in the game situation. The coach must remember that the learning process is just the same and that it may be necessary to adapt the progressions to concentrate upon the learning of these extra yet important factors.

A simple example will serve to illustrate this point: hitting the ball from the left side of the field to the right.

PROGRESSIONS FOR LEARNING THE SKILL

1. Hitting a stationary ball, emphasising body position (feet, shoulders, etc.).

2. Start behind and to the right of the ball, move to the left and around the ball to strike it to the right.

3. Start as above, but pull the ball back and across the front of the body using the reverse stick and then strike the ball to the right.

4. Trot with the ball on the open stick and then move around the ball as in 2 above and hit to the right.

5. Start as in 4 above, but then pull the ball across using the reverse stick as in progression 3.

6. Repeat 4 and 5, but begin with the ball on the reverse stick.

7. Repeat 2 to 6, but increase initial running pace with the ball and also run slightly diagonally left or right before performing the skills.

PROGRESSIONS FOR INTEGRATING THE SKILL

This involves the learnt skill along with learning how other factors influence the choice of technique. The other factors include the position of the opponents and of colleagues, the time available to perform the skill and how quickly the skill needs to be performed. The progression should be structured, using the pathways of stress described in the previous section, so that the learning can take place as well as the integration. In this situation it is very important that the coach sets the players the right tasks and provides the feedback concerning their decision making. This is a difficult but vital part of the coaching process – helping the player recognise cues and make correct responses so that skills and tactics can be successfully applied to the game situation.

The progressions might go as follows:

1. Dribbling and passing right to colleagues with passive defenders and plenty of space.

2. As above with the defender approaching up to five metres of the man with the ball, so narrowing the angle of his passes.

3. As in 1, but the defender running with the man in possession to add to the pressure, but allowing him to perform the skill.

4. As in 3, plus a more active defender looking to intercept the crossfield pass. There must be two passes available to the man in possession to give him a good chance of success.

5. As in 4, but put a passive defender on each of the two receivers so that the pass has to be more accurate.

6. As in 5, but give less space for the group to work in.

Further progressions may be devised according to the desires of the coach and the requirements of the players.

Finally, few players benefit from a learning or practice situation in which a low standard of expectation has been set. Coaches should not be afraid of setting high standards as long as they realise that standards must be attainable if they are to be motivating for players.

Learning Environment

There are three spheres which have an influence on the learning environment:

1. Facilities available.
2. Age and experience of players.
3. The coach.

The crucial element in any coaching session is that skill learning takes place (i.e. the players clearly improve in the desired areas) but it is also very important to have the maximum amount of participation possible, and a degree of enjoyment and variety in the practices. The mix of these ingredients in any one session will vary according to the three areas listed above.

FACILITIES

Little need be said about this, but a coaching session can be ruined at the outset by an attempt to coach something for which the facilities are totally unsuitable.

AGE AND EXPERIENCE OF PLAYERS

The greatest and yet most often overlooked differences a coach should account for are those between children and adults. Children have very different needs in the skill learning environment and, even within this collective term 'children', there are considerable variations with age that must be understood by the coach. (The characteristics of young players are outlined earlier in this chapter.)

THE COACH

The single most crucial area in any practice session is probably the coach. He can do more than either the facilities or the players to create the correct environment. More detail will be provided in the section on communication, but it is relevant to list here some of the attributes a good coach can bring to a learning environment.

Do:

* Be well organised and businesslike

in your approach.
* Be enthusiastic and convey the enjoyment factor.
* Understand the learning problems of the players.
* Err on the side of encouragement and positive feedback whenever possible.
* Give the players clear and attainable objectives.
* Give clear, concise and thoughtful instructions, whether planned or spontaneous.
* Demand that the players themselves find solutions to problems.
* Plan your session carefully but not rigidly.
* Evaluate yourself and your practices both during and after the session.
* Enjoy yourself and be yourself.

Do not:

* Be afraid of demanding high standards, although they must be relevant to the group.
* Be afraid of altering practices or progressions if the desired results are not being achieved.
* Be afraid to 'freeze' practices in order to illustrate or reinforce points of technique, and so on.
* Be afraid of questioning the actions of players.

SOURCES OF KNOWLEDGE

The best coaches are forever increasing their knowledge and although the increments will be smaller the more experienced the coach, it must not stop him studying the main sources of knowledge:

* Books and other publications.

* Coaching courses.
* Discussion.
* Personal playing experience.
* Observation.

These sources can be specific to hockey or include other sporting or coaching organisations – the coach can gain a great deal from investigating other sporting areas provided he is selective in his approach. There is a considerable amount of positive transfer across sporting divides if only we look carefully and intelligently.

The coach who fails to use his eyes and ears – *fails!*

COMMUNICATION

The ability to communicate is the second and equally important requirement of a coach, and in a team game such as hockey a successful coach is almost certainly a person who has mastered the skill of communicating. Without good communication learning cannot be achieved efficiently. Communication includes not only the immediate presentation of knowledge, but also the appropriate feedback after practice and the use of a variety of communicative skills.

It is important that the coach understands the areas of communication between himself and the players and the factors which influence the quality and success of communication.

The areas of communication are:

* Technical, tactical and physiological information.
* Concepts/principles which underpin team-work (for example co-operation and method of play).

* Organisation, discipline and motivation.

Factors influencing the quality of communication are:

* What is said – content and details.
* When it is said – timing/order of comments.
* How it is said – phrasing and tone of delivery.
* Whether it should be conveyed to individual, small group or everyone for best results.
* The quality and quantity of any demonstration, video or coaching technique (for example 'freezing' play) used to lead and/or support the verbal communication. 'Too much' is as bad as 'too little'!

CONCLUSION

The role of the coach is not an easy one due to the many functions he has to perform, the amount of knowledge he has to hold and the inevitable constraints influencing his programmes, but by its very nature it is a challenging one.

It will be appreciated that all the factors discussed in this chapter interact in a complex way to influence the quality of coaching, but perhaps underpinning the whole concept termed the 'art of coaching' is the simple statement: at all times use your common sense.

Finally, I repeat a few coaching howlers that may help you (all these are true!):

'If the worst comes to the worst, we'll have to play you.' (International team talk)

'... the reserves are O.K.; even Peter — has played sweeper for GB!' (International team talk)

'Stand with your feet closer apart.' (National coach)

'Half the time the centres are stopped, half the time they are missed and the other half they lead to goals!' (International player)

Fig 7   Samiullah (Pakistan) approaches the circle at speed, while England's Jimmy Duthie (No. 6) prepares to tackle and Malcolm Wilkinson tries to get back to help.

2 Methods of Play

The qualities of the players are more important than the playing system.

Everyone admires and enjoys watching a team which employs flowing moves and consistently high team and individual skills, but this method of play is the end product of many hours of thought and practice based upon the coach's harmonisation of the following factors:

* The philosophy of the coach.
* The qualities of the available players.
* The system or formation the team adopts.
* The roles assigned to the players within this formation.

PHILOSOPHY OF THE COACH

A great deal could be written here, but it is best kept on a very simple level. All coaches should know the kind of hockey team or players that ideally they are aiming to produce. These ideals are formulated and may be altered through experience, but while it is vital that a coach must work out his philosophy thoroughly so that it is not made up of ill-defined and rarely attainable concepts, he must also be honest to his players and himself as to how close to the ideal it is possible to get, given the relevant factors and how much success his philosophy produces (note – success need not be measured always by the number of wins).

The degree to which any coach can fulfil his philosophy depends upon:

1. The players available and the speed of turnover in personnel. These vary enormously at all levels in hockey, be it school, club, county, divisional or the various international age groups.
2. The time-scale available to the coach in which to develop the team and its players. Is it a school term, a playing season, six weeks to an important competition or a four year period up to the Olympic Games?

These two factors must be considered carefully by the coach as they will and must influence his objectives.

It would be impossible to categorise a philosophy accurately and fully as each coach's is slightly different, but I list below some of the major concepts that underpin coaching techniques and objectives and therefore provide the components of a coaching philosophy. I put them as questions which a coach might ask himself. What emphasis or priority do I put upon:

* Players expressing their skill?
* Players performing strictly to instructions?
* Players expressing their views?
* Attacking patterns?
* Defending patterns?
* Defenders only defending and attackers only attacking?
* Man to man or zonal marking?

Fig 8   Roderick Bowerman (Netherlands) attacks down the
right wing. Note the hand positions for both the reverse
and forehand stick play. (Netherlands v West Germany,
Champions Trophy 1982)

* Winning at any cost?
* Modifying a player's talents or accepting him as he is?
* Fitting the players to a system of play, or vice versa?
* Adapting to cope with the particular strengths of the opposition?
* Physical rather than skill training?
* Pressures applied by outside forces, for example by a headmaster or club chairman.

The answers will rarely be black or white, but rather a wide range of grey shades. However, when they are put together along with perhaps answers to even more questions, they do give a fairly clear indication of a coach's philosophy. Having formulated this, a coach is now able to set out specific objectives for a team, taking into account the resources and time-scale previously mentioned.

QUALITIES OF THE PLAYERS

Any method of play advanced by a coach must be very closely associated with the qualities of the players available but these qualities can, of course, be developed as a result of coaching. The characteristics that need to be assessed and developed by the coach and which can, therefore, influence the method of play are:

* Physical – speed; endurance; strength.
* Psychological – aggression; commitment; concentration level.
* Skills – strengths and weaknesses; preference for attack or defence.

If a single method of play is used over a long period of time, it is inevitable that new players capable of playing the basic roles associated with the system will continually appear. This happens in five of the six top hockey nations in the world: Netherlands, West Germany, Pakistan, India and Australia. In all these countries a single method of play dominates all levels of hockey. This is not the case in the other nation – Great Britain. It may be that the variety of methods in Great Britain actually has advantages in terms of teaching players to be adaptable, but it can also create problems in selecting players at the highest level.

Although it would be nice to think that all the coach needs to do is to work with the most skilful players and a successful side will emerge, we know that in reality this is not the case. Every successful squad has a wide variety of personalities, but it invariably includes natural leaders, one or two 'hard men' and 'play makers'. It is interesting that variety can create harmony and balance in a squad and this must not be overlooked.

SYSTEMS

The system used as the basis for the pattern of play is merely the formation used by the team, and the most common are: 5–3–2–1; 3–3–3–1–1; 4–2–3–1–1; and 4–2–4–1 (*Figs 9 to 12*). It must be remembered that these formations are far from rigid and merely form the foundation on which a pattern of play is developed. Their appearance in diagrammatic form is over-simplistic and the distribution of players as shown is rarely the case.

While there are basic playing principles which apply to all of these formations there are also differences which must be understood by both coach and player if a successful method of play is to be developed. The common factors are related to good playing habits, such as marking, covering, tackling, supporting, passing

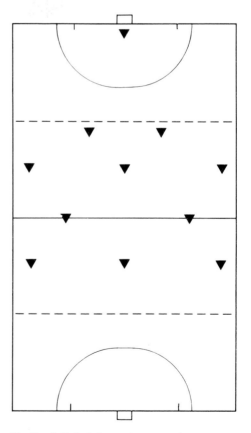

Fig 9   5–3–2–1 formation.

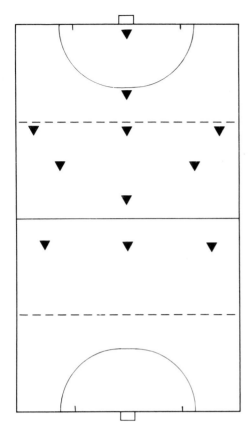

Fig 10   3-3-3-1-1 formation.

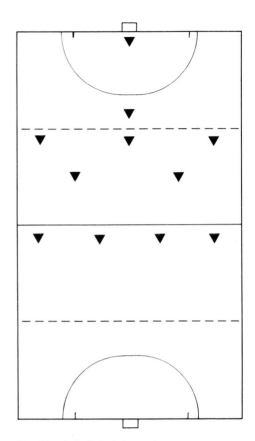

Fig 11   4-2-3-1-1 formation.

and shooting, while the major differences lie in the balance of the formation in terms of forwards, midfield and defenders and the degree of man to man and zonal marking generally found in each system. As a team becomes more sophisticated, it is quite likely that the characteristics of different formations can be used during phases of play, but these subtle alterations are closely related to the last factor influencing the pattern of play, the actual roles delimited by the coach.

Playing Roles Within a System

Formulating and altering the playing roles in a team formation is one of the most motivating aspects of coaching, as through this the coach is able to subtly alter the pattern of play to take account of strengths or weaknesses of the opposition or his own team. In order to achieve success it is important that the coach understands both the basic requirements of the roles he is formulating and the capabilities of the players he is directing to perform these roles. The skill is to bring both areas into harmony and to have run a coaching programme that has prepared the players sufficiently to take on the roles. A coach can safely ask a player to limit his role in a particular game, but it is dangerous to expect more of a player than he is capable of performing.

In order to assist in achieving harmony between players and playing roles, it is pertinent to look at the requirements for

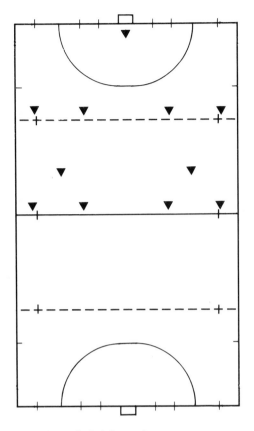

Fig 12　4-2-4-1 formation.

the basic roles. The table on pages 26 to 28 outlines these role requirements for the 5-3-2-1 and 3-3-3-1-1 systems.

In order to harmonise the basic requirements of the playing roles with the qualities of the players available, the coach must assess his players as objectively as possible (*see* Chapter 9). Having done this, the coach then has to formulate the playing roles. He may initially accept a rather limited role for a particular player, knowing that there may be the potential for further expansion as the player gains experience. The duties within each role will include both individual and group offensive and defensive responsibilities. As the roles are formulated, practised and developed, the pattern of play emerges, and on this foundation further refine-

ments can be made in order to make the pattern even more sophisticated and effective, to counter specific weaknesses or to cope with particular strengths of certain opposing teams.

What sort of changes might be made to the individual roles and the pattern of play to have an advantageous tactical influence upon the game? Remember that it is important that the changes do not upset your team's pattern to such an extent that there is no advantage gained.

1. An outstanding and key player may be marked man to man by a lesser player and, if done efficiently, the trade can be advantageous. There are, of course, variations on this theme and while they may not totally block the player out, they could reduce his effectiveness, without the need to totally relinquish one of your own players.
2. If a team has a particularly weak player then extra pressure can be applied if he is a defender, or little attention need be given to him if he is an attacker, thereby allowing his marker to concentrate more on an attacking role.
3. A poor passer of the ball on the opposition can be encouraged to have possession and then closed down.
4. A defender who likes to attack can be inhibited by a forward who is particularly good at both attacking and pressurising a defender in possession.
5. If an opponent tends to dribble a great deal, channelling him and isolating him from his support players can stifle his effectiveness.
6. Goalkeepers, like field players, have particular strengths and weaknesses. Some go down on the ground a great deal, some cause the ball to rebound a long way when saving with their legs and

PLAYING ROLE	OFFENSIVE REQUIREMENTS	DEFENSIVE REQUIREMENTS
Sweeper	Accurate short and long passes plus overhead passes. Intelligent and incisive running with and without the ball into attacking area. Ability to read the game. Confidence with the ball.	Tackling of all kinds. Closing down, shadowing, delaying, chanelling forwards who break through with the ball. Speed to get across to through ball and cover points of danger. Controlling all kinds of pass under pressure. Calm authority.
Full Back	As above.	As above. Working as a pair to mark CF, cover other defenders and close down a forward breaking through with the ball. Building up a sound defensive understanding with CH and WH.
Centre Back	As above but the marking responsibilities often restrict offensive moves to a minimum.	Marking and tackling have a high priority. Marking is man to man on CF and he must be fit and strong enough to cover the running of the forward and then make a tackle or interception, although the latter is usually restricted to crossfield passes/centres.
Right Half	Passing is a very high priority as RH is an easy position in which to receive the ball but a difficult position from which to distribute. Disguising and performing a wide variety of passes is important. Vision for attacking moves. Ability to beat an opponent and attack as an IF or wing.	Closing down and tackle using sideline as a colleague. Speed on the turn to counter pace of wing. Ability to work with other defenders in order to slow down and stop attacks on his flank and cover points of danger as opposition penetrate on the other flank.
Left Half	As above, plus: most passes have to be made from left to right and it is vital that the player is skilful at moving the ball and body into the correct position to do this. The offensive role is usually less demanding and the player must be capable of performing this more defensive role.	As above, plus: strength of reverse side tackle and interception.

PLAYING ROLE	OFFENSIVE REQUIREMENTS	DEFENSIVE REQUIREMENTS
Right and Left Half in 3–3–3–1–1	As above, except that their offensive roles are restricted by their marking responsibilities, although the RH is often used as a more attacking player to support the tight marking RM and the much freer CM.	As above, but man to man marking dominates.
Centre Half	Provides the principal link between defence and attack. Able to play a variety of passes to IFs so that latter can attack quickly. Ability to collect and give passes in complete 360 degree range so as to maintain momentum and/or change the point of attack. Retaining possession is a high priority in this role. Licence to support IFs and ability to attack opposing circle. Excellent poise, control and vision to set up attacks in open play and at restarts.	CH rarely has a specific marking role but the player must be aware of (a) stopping the direct pass to the CF down the centre of the field; (b) the danger of the crossfield pass between the IFs; defending IFs can help with this; (c) the opposing CH/CM pushing forward with ball; (d) channelling an opposing midfield player who is running with the ball; (e) covering the central area of the defensive circle and marking any opponent free in that area. Closing down, shadowing, channelling without being beaten are important requirements. Ability to recognise danger points in midfield and react accordingly. Positional play is very important as other defenders take their bearings from relative position of CH.
Centre Midfield	As above, but this role often has greater licence to move out of central area in order to act as the play maker. This requires more incisive qualities as noted for IF play and a high level of fitness. Offensive duties generally make up the larger proportion of the role.	As above, but the role demands closing down, pressurising and ball winning at danger points in midfield as other defenders (except sweeper) are marking man to man. Against another 3–3–3–1–1 formation, there is often a need to pay close attention to the opposing CM.

PLAYING ROLE	OFFENSIVE REQUIREMENTS	DEFENSIVE REQUIREMENTS
Inside Forward	Role of principal play maker in 5–3–2–1 system. Incisive dribbling, a wide variety of skills plus vision and deception are important abilities to link IF with surrounding players. Ability to receive passes from behind and retain possession in the tight confines of midfield. The workload requires high standards of fitness.	Primary role is to stop the ball getting to the opposing IF by marking alongside or in front of the player rather than behind him. Positioning and interception skills are very important, not only for IF but also the strikers as they work as a team particularly at restarts. Closing down players in midfield and tackling are also vital qualities.
Left and Right Midfield	If the emphasis is weighted towards marking tightly and winning the ball the offensive role is limited to the times when the ball is won or the team is dominating. After winning the ball simple, accurate passes are the priority, followed by support running. At restarts the ability to control the ball in the tight confines of midfield is vital as is the creation of space for himself or others if marking is man to man.	This is often the principal role of these players and therefore marking, closing down and tackling qualities are important. Man to man marking is usually expected of these players on opposition IF or midfield over whole defensive area. If one of these players is to be more attacking than the other then the rest of the defence has to be ready to compensate.
Strikers	Speed is a great asset for any winger or centre forward. Ability to make space if tightly marked, take a pass from behind and go forward, offer a lead to moves, beat defenders on either side, centre the ball accurately, and function in any of the front positions. Scoring goals is a major role of these men and therefore poise and balance in performing a variety of shots along with the aggressive attitude necessary in the cut and thrust in front of goal are important. When tight marking is experienced these men should be capable of making space for colleagues coming from deeper positions.	Tackling back, closing down and pressurising defenders along with good positioning at restarts can give considerable help to team defence.

feet, while others have a preference to save shots in the air or on the ground. It is important to take note of these characteristics and plan accordingly.

7. A specialist at overheads can be frustrated by rapid closing down by the forwards.

These are just a few of the alterations a coach could make to counter strengths and exploit weaknesses in the opposition, but the success of any individual role, pattern of play or tactic will depend upon understanding and discipline at both individual and team level.

3 Promoting and Developing On the Ball Skills

Skill is the combination of brain and body.

What is skill? It is the movement of body, stick and ball carried out by players within the constraints of the game of hockey (for example the rules) to overcome the problems facing them. The range of problems is vast, but includes such things as 'controlling the ball', 'scoring goals in a 5 v 4 situation' and 'team defence', i.e. the problem solving has to be done at individual, group and team levels. In addition to the obvious skill 'on the ball', it is important to recognise and develop skill 'off the ball', i.e. the movement and positioning of players, which is of paramount importance when defending and provides the support play to the man in possession in attack.

The teaching, learning and practising of these skills is, of course, of great importance in the development of hockey players as it provides them with a reservoir of knowledge along with technical and physical abilities to be used to find solutions to the problems facing them. Through practice a player develops a variety of solutions to a problem and is aware of the relative advantage of each. In a dynamic game such as hockey, there are so many factors influencing any one situation that it is unusual for a situation to be repeated identically and, therefore, it is impossible to say that there is only one solution to a problem. The art of coaching players is to balance the teaching of skill with the encouragement of players to use their own initiative in order to solve problems, and then to offer them the opportunity to practise making these decisions in increasingly stressful (or game-like) situations. This process introduces the concept of group and team play in which the individual has to subjugate some of his personal desires and place a higher priority upon group or team success. This demands that players find a solution to a situation that brings their team the greatest advantage or offers the opposition the least chance of success.

Let us not be naïve about hockey skills: they are far from easy! The various aspects of the game – small stick, small ball, use of only one side of the stick, no shielding of the ball, no use of the body, and so on – combine to make hockey perhaps the most difficult of the field games to master, yet one of the most challenging and rewarding. One of the principal aims of coaching is to break the complex structure into identifiable and more easily learnt components that can then be mastered in a progressive manner

Fig 13 Australia's Peter Hazelhurst cuts
(left) through the West German defence
(Peter, Bachmann and Stroder).

31

in order to achieve understanding and success in the performance of the whole skill or tactic.

The two principal concepts discussed in this introduction to developing skill – firstly that the skills of hockey need to be isolated and learnt and secondly that the game is dynamic and, therefore, players are required to use their skills to cope successfully with a wide variety of playing situations (problems) – coincide with the concepts of learning and practising put forward in Chapter 1.

The aim in the remainder of this chapter is to look at a number of basic individual and group skills and suggest ways in which to teach and develop them, rather than take every skill in the game. The basic formula can easily be transferred to other skills and tactics and in this way the coach can develop his own practices and progressions.

GRIPS *(Figs 14 & 15)*

As any movement of the ball must be done with the stick, it is important to have an understanding of the most efficient grips. Coaches should encourage all youngsters to play with the left hand above the right at all times. The left hand is the one which dictates the manipulation of the stick, whereas the right provides most of the power.

When the hands are apart the player has greater control of the ball in terms of manipulation, deception on the pass, speed of the pass and the variety of passes he can play. The restrictions to the player in this 'hands apart' position are that the stoop inhibits the running speed, the ball cannot be propelled at any great pace when passed and the player's vision is

restricted.

When the hands are together the player has greater vision and is able to hit the ball at considerable pace, but he loses the fine control of the ball, the range of passes he can make and the deception he can apply to the pass. The position of the right hand on the stick, therefore, varies according to the skill being performed when a player is in possession of the ball, but it is

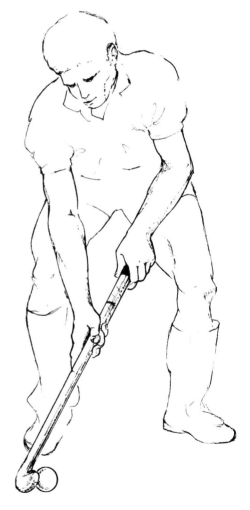

Fig 14 Forehand or open stick grip.

Fig 15 Reverse stick grip.

the top and is to the left of the ball. During this stick rotation, it is important that the right hand is relaxed and allows the stick to rotate.

It is not *wrong* to take the stick behind rather than over the top of the ball. The advantage of this method is that the ball can be moved from left to right, albeit diagonally forwards, without changing the grip and in a stronger position, with the blade of the stick following the ball. The movement of the arms has to be greater and the skill is probably harder to master than the over-the-top method, but it has been used successfully by a number of English players, notably Sean Kerly, Jon Shaw, Steve Batchelor and James Duthie. The weakness of this skill is that it cannot transfer the ball from left to right as quickly nor in as wide an arc as the over-the-top method. It is important that players and coaches understand these facts.

clear that a person strong in the wrists and forearms can gain advantages by having a higher right hand position.

The left hand grips the stick firmly near the top for all skills, but the grip does vary a little between dribbling, hitting and pushing/flicking. Good coaches must know these variations. The principal alteration is made when a player is running with the ball. In order to manipulate the ball from left to right the stick must be able to rotate in a 180 degree arc over the top of the ball. To do this the left hand grip must be rotated a little to the right, so the player can see two or three knuckles of the left hand when the stick is to the right of the ball and all four of his finger nails when the stick is rotated over

DRIBBLING

While any player in a game spends little time moving with the ball, when he does so it is often in critical situations and the degree of success he achieves can determine whether he has played well or not. He may be:

1. Drawing or beating a defender to open up an attacking opportunity in a congested area.
2. Beating a defender to exploit space to the side or behind him.
3. Drawing a defender to release a colleague into space.
4. Moving out of a congested area in defence.
5. Getting out of a very pressurised

situation in defence.

6. Moving rapidly through space with the ball.

The kind of dribble used by a player will vary according to the situation and it is, therefore, important to have a wide repertoire. Generally speaking, the greater the desired speed of the player, the more important it is to have the ball well in front of the body to allow the body and legs to achieve the most efficient running action possible. To attain maximum speed, it may mean that the ball is not on the stick all the time – although this can be done at relatively high speed, if the stick is held in the left hand with the ball to the left of the body or in the right hand with the ball on the right of the body. Greater control, with both hands on the stick, can only be achieved by reducing the speed of running or holding the right hand higher, and even then a player cannot run at maximum speed.

In all dribbling, the dexterity of the hands is vital as this determines how the ball is manipulated. In particular, it is advantageous to develop fast hand (and therefore stick) movements, as this means that although the ball is moved the stick is quickly back into contact with it for further manipulation.

Forehand Dribble

In the forehand or open side dribble, the ball is kept on the right-hand side of the body in front of and just outside the line of the right shoulder. The greater the control required, the closer the ball will be to the line of the feet and the slower the player will move, particularly if a rapid movement of the ball is likely to be necessary.

This type of close dribble is often used by players in congested areas of the field, particularly the circles. When there is greater space available the player may perform the same open side dribble but, by pushing the ball a little way ahead, the speed of running can be increased. This skill can be used to run the ball rapidly through space or into open space behind a stationary defender.

Indian Dribble

This type of dribbling provides a player with the ability to move the ball quickly to the left and right and is particularly useful for deception or a rapid change of direction. It is, therefore, of greatest advantage to a player when beating an opponent or working in a congested area, especially when accompanied by skilful body and stick feints. Particularly dangerous players are able to perform this Indian dribble with the ball:

1. In front of the body.
2. To the right of the right foot.
3. To the left of the left foot.
4. Moving from extreme left to extreme right.

Reverse Side Dribble

This is similar to the open side dribble when the ball is pushed ahead into space, except that only the left hand is kept on the stick. The ball is played well to the left and in front of the body and can be used very effectively by left wingers for outflanking the defence, but it requires the player to have great confidence on the reverse side.

Fig 16 The Dutch player uses the one-handed reverse stick dribble to get round the Pakistan full back.

Coaching Points for Dribbling

Coaches should make certain that they have a thorough understanding of the techniques of dribbling and are able to rectify the most common faults:

* Incorrect grip, particularly with the left hand.
* Hands not moving across the body with the stick in the Indian dribble.
* Right hand too low inhibiting both running speed and vision.
* Right hand too high reducing the control of the ball.
* Ball and stick too near the feet inhibiting running and vision.
* Stick too upright and not angled so that it is a straight extension of the left arm.

DRIBBLING PRACTICES

Use the most even surface possible, especially for beginners. Competitions and relays can easily be developed to make these practices more interesting.

Forehand Dribble

1. Run with the stick behind and in contact with the ball.
2. As above, but at different speeds.
3. As in 1, but accelerate and decelerate during the run.
4. As in 1, but lift the eyes as if to look for passes.
5. Run and push the ball a few yards ahead, so that the running speed can be increased.
6. As in 5, but look for passes during the

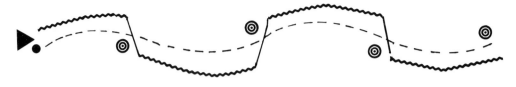

Fig 17

time the ball is not in contact with the stick.

7. Run the ball around obstacles placed in an inverted 'W' shape using only the open side dribble. This requires skilful movement of the legs, trunk, arms and hands and cannot be done at high speed.

Indian Dribble *(Figs 17 & 18)*

1. Move the ball continuously from left to right in the stationary position, gradually increasing the range of the movement.
2. Walk while performing the Indian dribble and then jog.
3. Run and perform the Indian dribble.
4. Run and dribble the ball with small side to side movements just outside the line of the right foot.
5. As in 3, but with the ball just outside the line of the left foot.
6. Repeat 3, 4 and 5 varying the speed of running.
7. Dribble through obstacles placed in a straight line. Vary the distances between the obstacles.
8. As in 7, but alternate between dribbling the ball to the left and right of the body *(Fig 17)*.
9. Use the Indian dribble to change the position of the ball very rapidly *(Fig 18)*. Dribble the ball and then use the reverse stick to change the direction of the ball suddenly and dribble along the new path.

Coaching points: move the ball first and let the stick and body follow. If the body weight is on the left foot as the reverse stick skill is performed, the player can move further and more rapidly after the ball. Body and stick feints practised now will help in the game.

10. As in 9, but the movement is now made from right to left. The sudden change of position of the ball is initiated

(a)

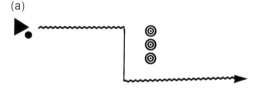

(b)

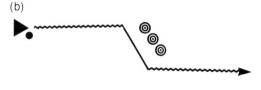

(c)

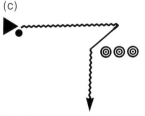

Fig 18

by the forehand stick and controlled on the reverse stick.

Coaching points: as in 9, but putting the body weight on the right foot as the skill is initiated helps the movement of the body.

PROGRESSIVE DRIBBLING PRACTICES

The following practices are some of the progressions a coach might use to increase the stress on the dribbling skills. I have developed the progressions along the three individual pathways of stress but the coach can progress exactly as he wishes, according to his objectives.

Skill Stress

All these practices can be done with obstacles or a passive defender.

FOREHAND DRIBBLE *(Figs 19 & 20)*

1. Run with the ball in an arc and then straighten up. The same skill can be practised left to right and right to left *(Fig 19)*.

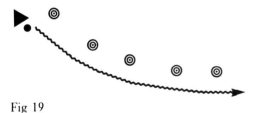

Fig 19

2. Run with the ball straight and then move in an arc *(Fig 20)*.
3. Repeat 1 and 2, but vary the speed: accelerate and decelerate.

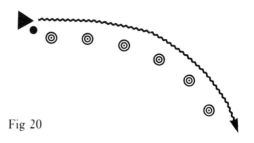

Fig 20

4. Run with the stick in contact with the ball, move the head of the stick to check the forward momentum of the ball and then accelerate with the ball.
5. As in 4, but after the ball has been checked, lift it forwards as if a low reverse stick tackle is blocking the way and accelerate with the ball.
6. Mix the skills in practices 1 to 5 together.
7. Repeat the skills in practices 1 to 5, but before the skill is begun receive a pass to the forehand stick from a variety of angles.
8. Repeat the skills in practices 1 to 6, but at the end of the move push, flick or hit the ball at targets as if you were passing or shooting.

INDIAN DRIBBLE *(Figs 21 to 26)*

1. Dribble through the slalom of obstacles placed in a straight line. Vary the player's speed and the distances between the obstacles.
2. As in 1, but with obstacles placed in a W formation. Emphasise the change of direction as the player rounds the cone.
3. Repeat 1 and 2 but emphasise: changes in speed of player; speed of stick movements; the distance the ball moves from side to side; body and stick feints.
4. Dribble to the left of the first cone *(Fig 21)* and then use the reverse stick to move

37

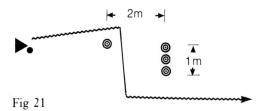

Fig 21

the ball rapidly to the right and dribble past the wall of cones. Emphasise efficient foot pattern, speed of stickwork and movement of the body. Add body and stick feints.

5. As in 4, but vary the distance the ball is moved from left to right, i.e. change the width of the wall.

6. As in 4, but alter the speed of running and consider what other adjustments have to be made to make the skill successful, for example timing of the movement, how sharply the player can change direction, and so on.

7. Repeat exercises 4, 5 and 6 but this time moving the ball from right to left and collecting it on the reverse stick.

8. Dribble towards the defender aiming for his right shoulder, move the ball across the body from right to left, and then move the ball sharply from left to right to go wide around the defender and then cut back in behind *(Fig 22)*. Experiment with the most efficient distance from the defender at which to start the move.

Fig 22

9. As in 8, but experiment with speed of player with the ball; speed of stick movement; range of movement of the ball from left to right; body and stick feints; foot pattern; and accelerating as you pass the

defender.

10. As in 8, but use a double movement from left to right *(Fig 23)*. This needs to be started further away from the defender.

Fig 23

11. Experiment as in 9.

12. Dribble towards the defender aiming for the left shoulder or even a little outside it, then move the ball rapidly to the left and collect it on the reverse stick before straightening the path of the ball and cutting back behind the defender *(Fig 24)*. Experiment as in practice 8.

Fig 24

13. Repeat the experimentation outlined in practice 9.

14. The defender shadows the attacker so that it is difficult for the attacker to beat him by going forward. The attacker overcomes this by pulling the ball back and across from left to right before running with the ball around the reverse stick side of the defender *(Fig 25)*. Experiment as shown in practice 9.

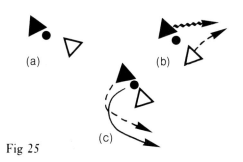

Fig 25

15. As in 14, but the attacker does not draw the ball across as far and then immediately plays it forwards past the feet of the defender *(Fig 26)*. Experiment as shown in practice 9.

Fig 26

16. These dribbling skills can be made even more complex by: demanding that the player controls a variety of passes before performing the skill; adding a pass or shot at the completion of the skill; demanding a pass forwards as the attacker is beating the defender.

Spatial Stress

As described in Chapter 1, this is a quite straightforward pathway of stress and the possible progressions illustrated below could be used for any of the dribbling skills.

1. Dribble through a defined area with only a few cones as obstacles, thereby providing maximum chance of successful practice.

2. Increasing the number of cones will increase the difficulty of the task.

3. Distributing the cones in a particular way will alter the kind of space available and influence the way the skill is performed. For example in *Fig 27* the player dribbles through the slalom, rounds the wall (or passive defender) on the reverse stick side, accelerates through space and then decelerates slightly to dribble through the group of cones with full control. This particular practice uses a combination of dribbling skills, but it could easily be modified to pressurise just one or two aspects of moving with the ball.

4. Reducing or increasing the size of the space in which to perform the skill is a principal method of introducing spatial stress, but the coach must be careful not to alter the shape or area to such an extent that players do not practise the intended skill but one that is more appropriate to the space available.

Competitive Stress

This pathway is obviously the one that takes the players closer and closer to the

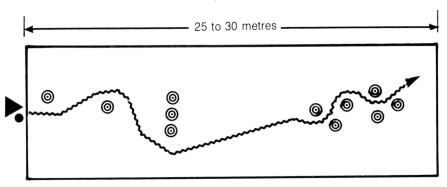

Fig 27

Fig 28 Hasan Sadar (Pakistan) attempts to beat two Australian defenders at pace in the 1984 Olympic semi-final. Notice how far ahead of his feet the ball and stick head are placed.

game situation, and inherent in this progression is the fact that the more competitive the practice, the more difficult it is to have the emphasis upon only one aspect of the game, for example dribbling. The coach must also be aware that the very nature of the competitive practice may result in the skill in question not being practised very much and it is important to plan these progressions carefully. It does not really matter if other skills come into the practice and even dominate it, provided the coach is aware of the situation and is not expecting something that is unobtainable from the particular competitive practice. All too often this pathway of stress is rushed along, with the result that the players are ill-equipped to perform the skill or tactic in the very competitive environment en-

forced upon them.

Here are some possible progressions for dribbling. (Note: I would put very little spatial stress on these practices, particularly as they become more competitive. Space is essential for successful dribbling practice.)

1. Non-competitive relays practising the skills, using cones as obstacles if necessary.
2. As in 1, but make the relays competitive. Make certain that the skills are being done properly.
3. Rapid repetition of the skill by a player introduces the fatigue factor that will be experienced in the more competitive situation.
4. Introduce one or more passive defenders to give the performer a better idea of

how opponents will respond to his moves. This phase will help the player develop important aspects of the skill, such as making the defender move in a particular way, timing his own change of direction, how and where to position the ball and body during the movement in relation to the defender.

It is important that the passive defenders follow the coach's instructions. For example, they might be told to:

* Make the dribbler go on your reverse side (or open side).
* Open up your reverse side and place a flat reverse stick tackle to encourage the attacker to lift the ball over it.
* Run back with the man so that he must keep the stick close to the ball.
* Let the man beat you, then chase him so that he can practise cutting across your path as he passes you.
* Jab tackle to make the man judge the timing of the move.

There are many more conditions that can be imposed to ensure that the right skills are being practised.
5. Small-sided conditioned games, for example 5 v 3 (five attackers against three defenders). The attackers score by dribbling the ball under control over the opponents' goal line. The defenders score every time they gain possession by a tackle or interception. The practice area should be about 25×20m, and the goal line is the full width of the area.

CONTROLLING THE BALL

In any passing game the ability to control the ball is a vital ingredient in a successful side. Controlling the ball means collec-

ting the pass and positioning it for the next predetermined movement as quickly as possible. This may require the ball to be stopped 'dead', but more often than not the advanced player repositions the ball during the movement to give himself space and time for any subsequent play.

General Principles

1. The player's eyes and stick should be along the line of the ball for as long as possible.
2. The receiver must watch the ball right onto the stick.
3. The right hand is the key to the cushioning of the ball so that it can be repositioned as the receiver requires. The right hand needs to be strong but able to make the stick 'give' at the time of impact.
4. It is very difficult to control the ball if the stick moves across the line of the ball, but much easier if the player allows the ball to come onto the stick.
5. The receiver should always try to be in a balanced position when collecting a pass. This can be done even though the player is running, although the skill becomes much more difficult the faster the player is moving.
6. The receiver should lift his eyes to assess the situation before or after he controls the ball, *not* as he performs the skill.

Controlling Ball Passed from Left

ON THE FOREHAND STICK
(Figs 29 & 30)

The receiver usually adopts one of the following body positions. In the first *(Fig 29)*, the player's chest faces the ball and the ideal point of control is between

41

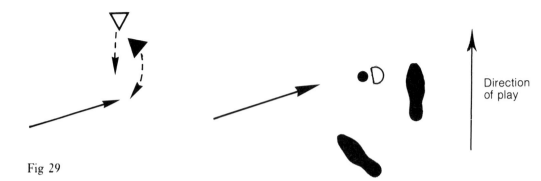

Fig 29

the feet or by the right foot. This technique allows the player to get his eyes, stick and body behind the line of the ball, giving himself maximum opportunity to control the pass, but because this position cannot be taken up while moving forwards emphasis must be put upon quickly repositioning the ball and body immediately after the ball has been controlled. This skill is often used by players when they have come back quickly towards their own goal to escape from a tight marking opponent.

The second method *(Fig 30)* is only slightly different but it allows the receiver to be moving forward as he controls the ball. As the player is running forward, the chest cannot be turned much towards the ball but the eyes and stick get in line with the pass through the natural forward lean of the body. The ball is controlled inside the line of the left foot and it is important to get the foot pattern in harmony with the control, so that the player is able to perform a subsequent predetermined movement.

The choice of which method to use will depend upon a variety of factors including the type of pitch, the speed and quality of the pass, the position of the opposition and the position and movement of colleagues.

ON THE REVERSE STICK *(Fig 31)*

All players must be able to control passes on the reverse side, even when they come from the left, as not every pass will be totally accurate or it may be the only line of pass available to the passer. (For technique, *see* the section on controlling the ball passed from the right.) The important point for players receiving these passes is that they must turn quickly to face the opposition so that they do not obstruct. Advanced players have found that it is possible to use a pass from left to right aimed deliberately at the reverse stick without producing obstruction.

As the attacker moves away from the defender the ball is passed to his reverse side and he turns anticlockwise as he controls it and then dribbles upfield *(Fig 31)*. This is a highly skilful move and

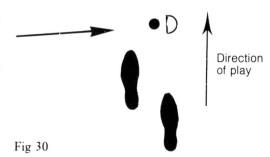

Fig 30

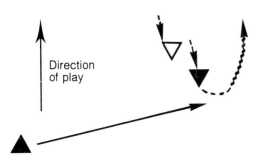

Fig 31

right shoulder faces the ball, the head of the stick is on the line of the pass and the eyes (through the natural forward lean of the body) get as close to the line of the pass as is possible. The ball is usually controlled in line with the left foot or outside it, as this allows the forward momentum to be continued.

With practice players should be able to control the ball on the reverse side at considerable speed and with the left hand only if the ball is passed well ahead of them.

requires excellent timing to avoid obstruction. Pakistan inside rights use it frequently against tight marking opponents.

Controlling Ball Passed from Right

ON THE REVERSE STICK *(Fig 32)*

This is normally used when the player is going forward and has space in front of him, as it is easier to control the ball if it is placed a metre or so ahead of his feet. The

ON THE FOREHAND STICK
(Figs 33 & 34)

Players often collect passes from the right on their forehand stick and this can be done not only in the stationary position but also while they are moving towards or away from the opponents' goal.

1. *Controlling while stationary or moving away from the goal.* This skill is often used in a congested area (for example the

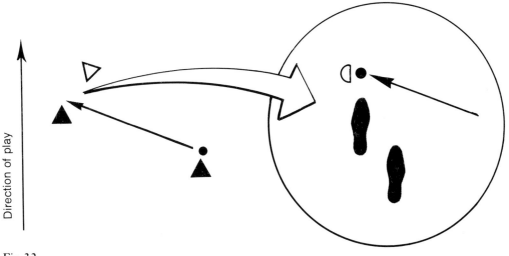

Fig 32

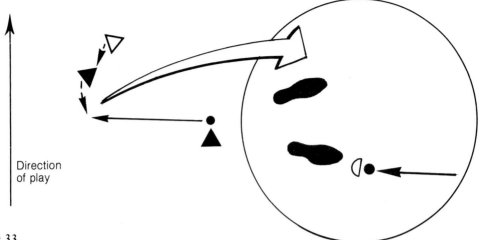

Direction of play

Fig 33

circle) or when a player is being marked tightly. The player moves away from the defender and receives the pass from the right onto his forehand stick. At the moment of control the player must ideally be well balanced with knees slightly bent, feet apart with the chest facing the ball, although generally the body weight tends to be over the right leg *(Fig 33)*. The ball is controlled in front of or outside the right foot.

It is very important that the receiver develops nimble footwork, body movement and skilful ball positioning to minimise the chances of the defender being able to tackle him.

2. *Controlling while moving forward.* In this situation the receiver while moving forward twists the upper part of his body towards the ball and collects the pass on the forehand stick quite close to his feet *(Fig 34)*.

These forehand techniques are particularly useful when players are closely marked, when the area is congested, or when possession with the ball in a strong position to pass or dribble is a high priority.

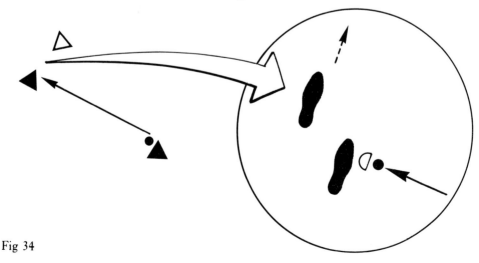

Fig 34

Controlling Ball Passed From Front *(Fig 35)*

This normally takes place when the opposition have had possession and a player is intercepting a pass. Ideally the ball is controlled with a near vertical stick on the forehand, either between the feet or close to the right foot *(Fig 35)*. Players also ought to be capable of moving the stick to the left and controlling the ball passed close to their left foot without having to turn the stick over to the reverse side.

Coaches and players should take account of the advantages and disadvantages of this skill and use it accordingly. It is excellent for tackling, intercepting, controlling an inaccurate pass and deflecting passes towards goal but is of little use when fluent movement of player and ball is a high priority.

Controlling Ball from Behind

When a team is attacking, many passes are received from behind and players need to

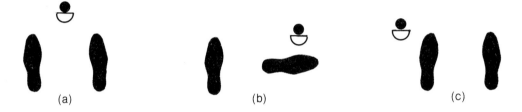

(a)　　　　　　　　(b)　　　　　　　　(c)

Fig 35

When the reverse stick control is required in these situations, the skill is the same as described in the section on controlling a pass from the right with the exception that the player is likely to be stationary or moving slowly. On artificial pitches the ball runs much more smoothly and this allows players to use a more horizontal stick position when required and also to collect the ball more easily while moving forward.

At this point it is relevant to point out that while controlling the ball with the stick almost horizontal to the floor is a very useful skill, the low position of the body does not facilitate fluent body movements immediately after the ball is controlled as the player has to raise his centre of gravity (i.e. stand up more) before he can twist or turn quickly.

be able to control these not only when they are stationary but, more importantly, while they are moving towards the ball, away from the ball or across the line of the ball on either the forehand or the reverse stick.

ON THE FOREHAND STICK
(Figs 36 to 38)

1. *While moving towards the ball* This is often used to evade a tight marking defender. The forward runs towards the ball and usually controls it between the feet or beside the right foot, depending upon the predetermined subsequent move *(Fig 36)*.
2. *While moving away from the ball* In this case the receiver is running in the same direction as the pass but at a slight

45

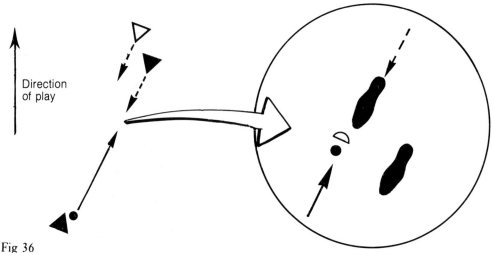

Fig 36

angle to the ball to allow the player to look over the left shoulder at the pass and bring the stick across and in line with the pass *(Fig 37)*.

3. *While moving across the line of the ball* The major difficulty in this skill is that the eyes and stick cannot be on the line of the pass until immediately before the point of control, so the player has to concentrate particularly well to consis-

tently succeed. The faster the player and the ball are moving, the more difficult the skill becomes. Control takes place between the feet or close to the line of the right foot, with the left shoulder facing the ball *(Fig 38)*. The closer the defender, the more important the subsequent movement of ball and/or player if obstruction is to be avoided.

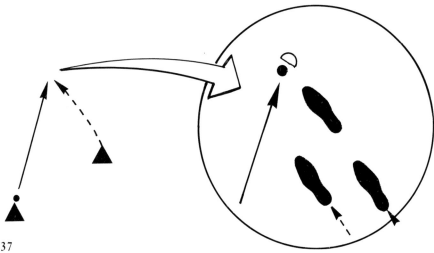

Fig 37

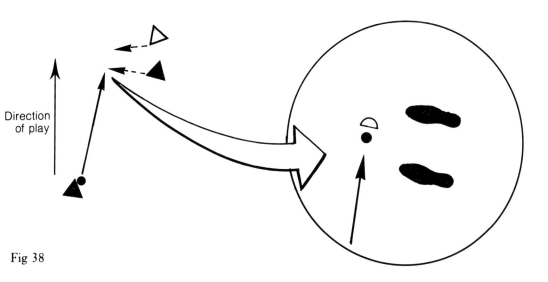

Fig 38

ON THE REVERSE STICK
(Figs 39 & 40)

1. *While moving away from the ball* The receiver runs at an angle to the line of the ball in order to be able to look over the right shoulder at the approaching ball, while allowing the right hand to come across the front of the body to position the stick in line with the pass *(Fig 39)*.

The ball is collected in advance of the feet so that the forward run can be continued.
2. *While moving across the line of the ball* This is very similar to the previous skill, with the exception that the angle of the run is closer to 90 degrees to the line of the ball *(Fig 40)*. It is, therefore, a more difficult skill to perform at speed *(see* notes on forehand skill).

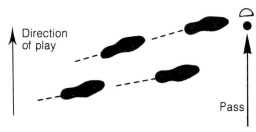

Fig 40

Practices for Controlling the Ball

In all these practices the good coach must understand the position and movement of feet, trunk, head, body weight, arms and stick so that he can teach inexperienced

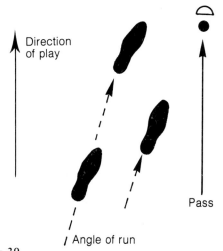

Fig 39

players the basic skills and yet be able to guide the more advanced players through a series of progressions that would prepare them for high quality performance under increasing degrees of stress.

The following series of practices are only a few of the hundreds that a coach can develop according to the players being coached, the facilities and the objectives of the particular session. It can be argued that *every* practice is a practice for control; while that is true, I have tried in this series not to put a high emphasis upon any other aspect of the game.

1. Two players, facing each other in a stationary position, push and control the ball on the forehand stick (emphasise techniques). The distance between them can be varied, but five to ten metres is ideal.
2. As in 1, but control the ball on the reverse stick.
3. Repeat 1 and 2, but with two balls moving round a rectangle made up of four players.

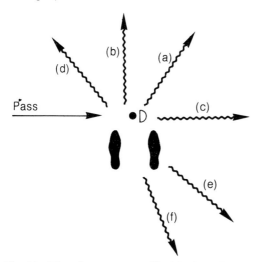

Fig 41   The player moves off with the ball; (a) to (f) indicate the degree of difficulty.

4. Repeat 1 to 3, but vary the type of passes given, for example push, hit and lifted pass.
5. As in 1, but ask the players to control the ball with their left shoulder towards the line of the pass, and then move the ball and themselves in the directions shown in *Fig 41* with as little delay as possible. Stick and body feints can be added to these moves.
6. As in 5, but control the ball on the reverse stick and move with it as shown in *Fig 42*.

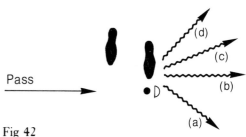

Fig 42

7. Repeat 5 and 6, but pass the ball by hitting it.
8. Practise receiving the ball from behind on the forehand stick and moving on in the direction shown in *Fig 43*. Increase the speed of running and passing as the players' confidence increases.

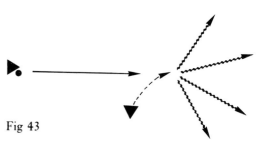

Fig 43

9. Practise receiving the ball from behind on the reverse stick and moving in the direction shown in *Fig 44*. Increase the

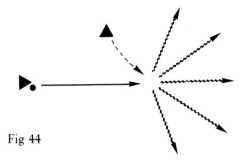

Fig 44

speed of running and passing as in 8.

10. Repeat 8 and 9, but with the receiver running across the line of the pass.

11. Repeat 5, but the receiver runs towards the passer before he receives the ball.

12. Passive and then active defenders can be introduced to put greater stress on the performer.

13. The receiver can be asked to perform another skill after any of the movements in practices 5 to 11, for example to pass to particular targets, beat another defender or shoot at goal.

14. Moving in pairs up and down the pitch, practise controlling the ball from the right, from the left and from behind. This introduces an emphasis upon the quality of the pass because both the passer and the receiver are moving and it is this vitally important skill of passing that the next section is concerned with.

In conclusion to this section on practices for control, I must add that innumerable progressions are possible if the coach makes use of the pathways described in Chapter 1 and his imagination.

PASSING

Passing and control of the ball are without doubt two of the most important aspects of hockey as they provide the principal method of moving the ball into the shooting area. The only other way to propel the ball there is by dribbling it and this cannot be done as quickly as by passing movements. It is, therefore, imperative that players learn to pass and receive the ball early in their playing careers so that they can begin to understand the passing options open to them.

The types of passes most often talked about by coaches and players are *square*, *through* and *angled* and these are shown in *Figs 45 to 47*.

The most important aspect concerning a pass is that it is successful and to make sure of this both ends of the pass, the passer and the receiver, must be in harmony. The player passing the ball must utilise his skill in positioning the ball and himself so that he is able to perform the correct pass, while the receiver has to make use of his knowledge of moving into space and his skill in controlling the ball to offer the passer a target for the pass and to make it successful. The first portion of the receiver's skill, moving into space, is an 'off the ball' skill and the reader should study the section on this in the next chapter before setting up passing practices.

Anyone who has watched hockey will have seen that making successful passes is not always easy and when the factors that influence any one pass are studied, the complexity of the operation becomes even more evident – these factors are shown in *Fig 48*. All these factors influence the decision of the man in possession as to whether he passes or not,

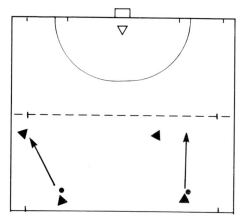

Fig 45   Through passes are made approx-
imately parallel to the sidelines.

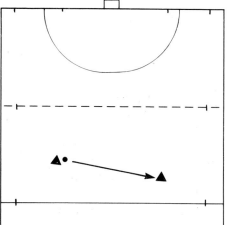

Fig 46   Square passes are made at approx-
imately 90° to the sidelines.

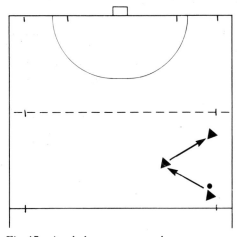

Fig 47   Angled passes are made at
acute angles across the field.

which pass he makes and when he makes
the pass. Coaches must remember that
only the man in possession can make this
decision and practices are the environment in which players must learn both
this decision making process and the skill
of helping the pass be successful by
intelligent movement both with and without the ball.

The art of coaching the complexities of
passing is to build it up in stages so that
the players are always moving from
known to unknown and simple to complex. The first stage has to be the development of one or more of the passing
skills, although it is normal to combine
this with the basic concepts of controlling
the ball and linking the passer and the
receiver so that players are progressing in
three areas simultaneously, albeit probably at three different speeds.

The basic passing skills are: pushing;
hitting; and flicking (aerial pass). I do not
propose to go through the techniques for
each of these skills in detail but to state the
differing types of each stroke that players
should be able to perform and the major
coaching points. All the passing skills are
primarily side-on skills; that is, whenever
any of them are performed, one of the
player's shoulders tends to point in the
direction of the pass–on forehand strokes
it is the left shoulder and on reverse stick
strokes it is the right shoulder. Deception
is an important aspect of all passing, as it
can disguise the intended direction of a
pass, but the coach must be careful only to
introduce this after the player has mastered the art of passing accurately. A general point to stress is that effectiveness is
more important than perfect technique
and coaches should refrain from altering
a player's effective method unless it is
particularly inhibiting his development.

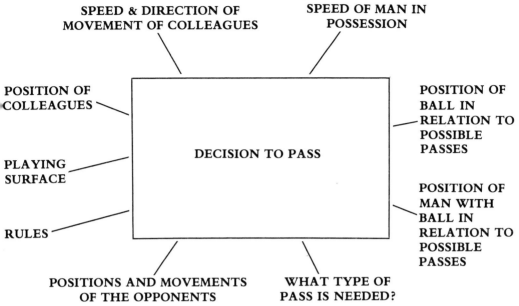

SPEED & DIRECTION OF MOVEMENT OF COLLEAGUES

SPEED OF MAN IN POSSESSION

POSITION OF COLLEAGUES

POSITION OF BALL IN RELATION TO POSSIBLE PASSES

DECISION TO PASS

PLAYING SURFACE

POSITION OF MAN WITH BALL IN RELATION TO POSSIBLE PASSES

RULES

POSITIONS AND MOVEMENTS OF THE OPPONENTS

WHAT TYPE OF PASS IS NEEDED?

Fig 48

Pushing

This is the most commonly used passing skill, particularly on artificial surfaces, as it allows the player to pass quickly in a wide arc without any great indication of the actual direction, although the speed of the ball is not as great as a hit.

FOREHAND PUSH

1. The ball is to the right of the body and towards the left (front) foot.
2. The hands are apart with the right hand below the left.
3. The legs are slightly bent with the body over the ball.
4. The left leg steps forward towards the target and the power comes from this forward movement of the body and the action of both of the arms.
5. The right arm drives forward rapidly while the left pulls backward so causing the head of the stick to accelerate.
6. Keep the eyes on the ball throughout

the skill.
7. Good footwork is the key to early success.

Players should practise controlling the ball and pushing firstly to targets throughout a 360 degree range, and secondly with the right foot forward.

REVERSE STICK PUSH

This is usually a short pass either square or backward from left to right. It is performed with the toe of the stick as an extension to the reverse stick movement of the ball in the Indian dribble.

If the ball is to be played backward, then the player must position the ball and body in such a way that there is a clear path for the ball.

Hitting

This skill is used when it is important that the ball travels at high speed, perhaps to reach a colleague some distance away, to penetrate a gap before it can be intercepted or to beat the goalkeeper.

WITH WEIGHT ON LEFT FOOT

This is the most commonly used method of hitting, but it is important that players learn to strike the ball hard, accurately and smoothly in a number of situations: when the ball is stationary; when the ball and player are moving; when the player has to move around the ball to strike it to the right; and when the player has to move around a moving ball to strike it to the right.

The principal coaching points are:

1. The shoulders are side-on to the direction of the pass, with the left shoulder facing the target at the start of the swing.
2. Body weight transfers onto the left leg at the point of impact.
3. The left leg is slightly bent but braced at the time of impact.
4. The stick is taken back by the arms and the arms are straight at the point of impact.
5. The ball is level with the left foot at impact.
6. The stick follows through along the line of the ball but then cuts away to the left and is restrained from following through too high.
7. Greater speed of the head of the stick at impact, and therefore greater power, can be obtained by utilising wrist action and more rotation of the trunk in the backswing.
8. Disguise in the pass can be achieved by skilful wrist action which opens or closes the face of the stick just before the point of impact.

WITH WEIGHT ON RIGHT FOOT
(Fig 49)

The techniques are exactly the same except that the right foot will be nearer the ball than the left and the body weight will be over that foot at the point of impact. This skill is more difficult but players should aim to be able to hit passes off the right foot both from left to right and right to left.

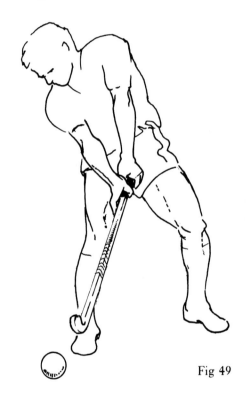

Fig 49

Flick

This skill is used to flick the ball in the air; skilled players can send the ball over fifty metres in the air. The technique is similar to the push, but the ball is usually a little further ahead so that the stick can get under the ball more easily and consequently the body position is lower. The power comes from the use of the arms and wrists and it is important that the body weight and stick move forward with the ball during the performance of the skill. Players with strong wrists and arms have a considerable advantage in the execution of the flick.

Beginners should gradually develop their skill by flicking the ball at ever higher targets until they can clear the goal, and then continue to aim to clear that kind of obstacle while moving further away from it.

After the stationary flick has been mastered players should attempt the same skill while the ball is moving.

Other skills such as the reverse stick scoop, hit and flick are all attributes for the better players, and talented performers are always coming up with innovative passing and shooting skills. Coaches should not discourage these, but seek to perfect and utilise them where relevant to the game situation.

PASSING PRACTICES

I have split these practices into two groups, the first orientated primarily to grooving the passing skills and the second to introduce concepts such as the movement of the receiver, the position of the opposition and the timing of the pass, i.e. to take the practices towards the game situation. I must emphasise, however, that any progression shown here is merely my progression and certainly not the only one nor the best one. I have no doubt that you will find different and and better progressions and indeed you should, because although the practices for

grooving the stroke may be relevant and repeatable for all groups, the progressions towards the game situation must be continually adapted by the coach to fit the specific needs of the players he is coaching at that particular time. The tinkering may only appear to be minor but it is the difference between a finely tuned engine and one that is misfiring!

Grooving the Skill

The following areas of practice can be applied to all the passing skills. Remember that if the skill is complex (for example moving around the ball on the run to hit from left to right), it should be broken down into smaller units and grooved accordingly. These practices *do not* account for this.

1. Practise the skill while stationary or moving slowly. This should not be done for long as the skill must be integrated with other bodily and ball movements. This kind of work can be done in pairs, threes or fours, using all kinds of actual practices but the emphasis must be on technique.
2. Use the skill to distribute the ball to a number of receivers in as wide an arc as the coach decides – 90 or 180 degrees or more. Groups of four with one player distributing to the other three is organisationally sound, especially if there are two balls with which to work.
3. As in 2, but the distributor moves forwards or sideways with the ball before he distributes it.
4. As in 2, but the distributor controls a pass before he distributes.
5. As in 2, but the distributor collects the ball from a few metres behind him before he distributes it.

6. As in 2, but the man dispossesses a passive attacker before he distributes.

7. As in 2, but the distributor is pressured by an opponent while he is passing. The aim must not be to tackle him.

8. As in 2, but there are one or two players who try to intercept the pass to the receivers. The number and position of these players must be thought out carefully to give the distributor a fair chance of succeeding.

In addition, it is possible to integrate two or more of these practices to put even greater stress upon the passer, and the receivers can be asked to control the ball in a particular way so that they gain more from the practices (refer to the section on controlling the ball).

Advanced Passing Practices

These practices progress towards the game situation. During the early progressions emphasis should be placed upon the following coaching points:

1. The movement of the player without the ball.
2. Providing a target for the passer.
3. The timing of the movement in relation to the space to be used and the man in possession.
4. The timing, position and speed of the pass.
5. The passer must try always to be in balance even when moving with the ball.

Later, as defenders are introduced, the coach should emphasise more advanced coaching points, such as:

6. The movement of the player with the ball and the use of deception to help create space for the pass.

7. How the position and movement of defenders influence the pass.

In many of the practices I have set problems without offering answers. It is important that you as coaches and players think these things out for yourselves rather than be spoon-fed all the time. Very often the practice itself is not as important as the concepts and problems which it throws up at players and coaches alike.

The following practices are illustrated using grids 10 × 10 metres, but if this space is restrictive use two grids per pair or areas of a pitch.

Practices for moving in advance of the ball and collecting a pass on the forehand and reverse stick (Fig 50).

1. Time the run and pass so that the ball and player A arrive at the same time. Player A must control the ball and continue running with it for a few metres as he might in a game.

2. As in 1, but demand that he controls the ball and then changes direction and continues dribbling in the new direction.

3. Time the run so that A arrives close to the intended point of control, settles and then the pass is sent quickly to his stick. A controls the pass and continues in the general direction of the pass (i.e. as if going upfield).

4. Repeat 1, 2 and 3 using various types of pass from B to A.

5. Repeat 1, 2 and 3 emphasising the placement of the pass from A to B. How is the timing for the second pass influenced by B controlling the ball on his reverse rather than forehand stick?

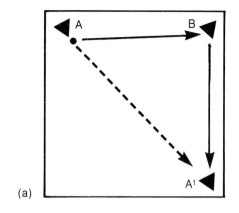

(a)

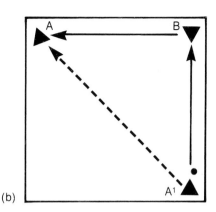

(b)

Fig 50

Practices for receiving a pass (square, backward of square or angled forward) from the right on both the forehand and reverse stick (Fig 51).

1. Run through the practice passing the ball backward, square and forward to both reverse and forehand stick in a definite sequence (emphasise timing to maintain forward movement). Vary the type of pass used.

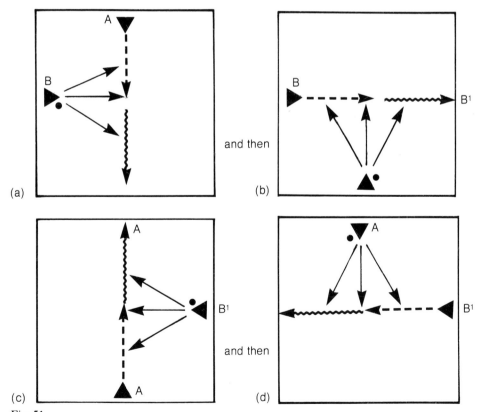

(a)

and then

(b)

(c)

and then

(d)

Fig 51

2. Repeat 1, but only for the square and backward passes and ask the receiver to accelerate as he controls the ball.

3. Repeat the practice using only the forward pass to forehand and reverse stick and ask the receiver to accelerate before receiving the ball. Which method of collecting the ball allows the receiver to run faster? When can this be used?

4. Repeat 1, 2 and 3 but have the player giving the pass moving slowly
   (a) in the same direction as the receiver *(Fig 52)*,
   (b) slightly across the pitch, forward, towards or away from the receiver.

All these changes require subtle variations in the timing of the move.

Practices for receiving a pass (square, backward of square or angled forward) from the left on the forehand stick.
Repeat all the practices above for receiving a pass from the right but the sequence will be that player A starts with the ball *(Fig 53)*.

Practices for passing forward to a player who is coming towards the ball and receiving it on the forehand.

1. Passing forward to forehand stick (right to left) *(Fig 54)*.
   (a) Player B initiates the move and A passes the ball so that the receiver can control it on his forehand stick. He should then move gently forward with the ball.
   (b) Repeat (a) but wait until the receiver has moved into space and settled before passing the ball quickly to his stick.
   (c) Repeat (a) and (b) but vary the type of pass used.
   (d) Repeat (a), (b) and (c) but vary the

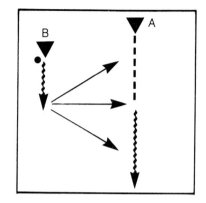

Fig 52

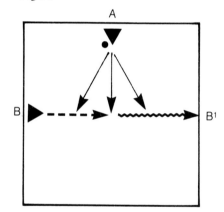

Fig 53

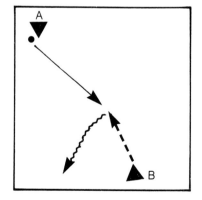

Fig 54

angle and distance of the pass.
(e) Repeat (a) to (d) but with A moving with the ball (forwards, sideways and backwards).
2. Passing forward to forehand stick (left to right). Repeat above practices but with the pass being played forwards and from left to right.

INTRODUCING OBSTACLES

Repeat all or some of the practices above but put obstacles in the way of the passes, so that both passer and receiver have to take account of them in the timings of their running and giving of the pass. A few cones are sufficient. (Refer also to the practices for receiving a pass (square, backward of square or angled forward) from the right on both the forehand and reverse stick.)

INTRODUCING DEFENDERS

The introduction of a defender into the practices will not only help re-emphasise the importance of the coaching points 1 to 5 (see page 54) but will also make the players aware of the importance of adapting their own movements so that a pass can still be made irrespective of the position and movements of the defenders (coaching points 6 and 7 on page 54). This kind of practice is a vital part of the transition to the game situation.

Initially one defender can be utilised against two attackers seeking to make a pass. This defender can be placed to pressurise either the man in possession or the receiver, and the degree of pressure can be altered at the discretion of the coach.

1. In *Fig 55*, A and B are trying to

combine to make either pass 1 or pass 2 succeed. The defender is passive at first. The skill of the attackers is to understand one another's movements and perform in harmony. To do this they need to solve various problems:

* How can A move with the ball to help create the opportunity for each pass?
* How does the position of the defender affect the situation? Get the defender to vary his position in relation to the two players.
* When is deception best used and can the receiver recognise it?
* What is the response of the man with the ball if the defender is 5–8 metres away?
* Can B initiate the move and A respond by moving with the ball to make the pass possible?

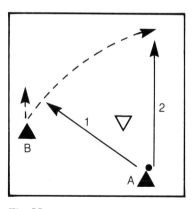

Fig 55

If the defender is allowed to become fully active, then it may be beneficial to allow the attackers to get the ball to the end of the area using one of the passes and/or a dribble, as this will introduce the concept of using a colleague as a dummy to beat a defender.

2. Repeat practice 1 but this time the ball is starting in a different position *(Fig 56)*.

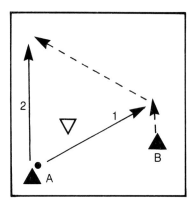

Fig 56

3. Combine practices 1 and 2 and play 2 v 1 but passes must be forward.

Note: These are not practices for the defender and so the player furthest from the goal line must be pressured (i.e. A) at the start.

4. A and B are trying to combine to beat the one defender and take the ball over the end line by dribbling and passing square or backward of square. At the beginning of each practice the defender may start anywhere on the centre line of the area.

*   How can the man in possession set up a successful move?
*   When can he dummy the defender and dribble through?
*   How does the man off the ball move? When does he change pace?
*   How do the attackers react to a defender who approaches them; stands still; backs away?

Repeat the practice but with B starting with the ball.

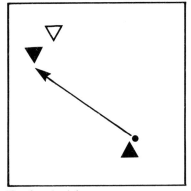

Forehand stick.

or

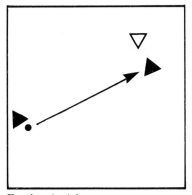

Forehand stick.

or

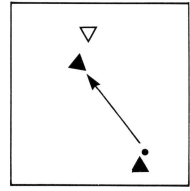

Reverse stick.

Fig 57

When an attacker moves back to receive a pass it is often because he is being marked, and to practise the timing of this move the defender must pressurise the receiver rather than the passer.

5. A and B are combining to pass the ball safely to B so that he is able to take the ball in balance, turn and go forward with it (*Fig 57*).

* How does the receiver initiate the move?
* Where is the best position to receive the ball if space has been made?
* Does running towards the ball help? If so, in what circumstances?
* How can the receiver get the ball beyond the defender when the latter is still very close?
* How does the distance the pass has to travel affect the pace required on the pass?

6. Begin exactly as in practice 5, but this time B deliberately allows the defender to stay close to him and the change of pace is used to go forward again to receive a forward pass (*Fig 58*).

* What are the cues for the man in possession?
* How hard must the pass be?
* Could the receiver cut across the front of the defender in (a) and (b). If so, under what circumstances?

The introduction of two defenders makes the problem even more complex for the attackers, but there are ways in which the man in possession can keep the ball going forward and therefore the defenders backward. In these practices the defenders ought to be passive to start with, to ensure success.

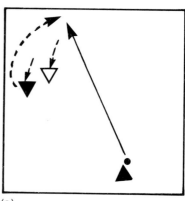

(a)
or

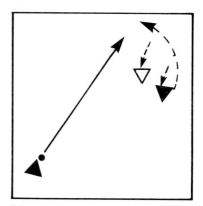

(b)
or

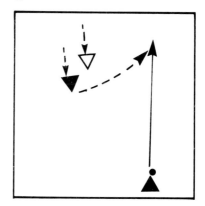

(c)

Fig 58

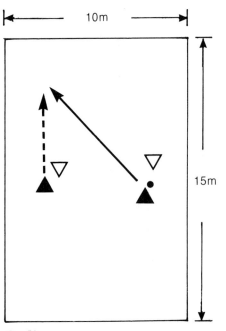

Fig 59

(b) If one of the defenders positions himself incorrectly, the man in possession may be able to create an opening as he has space to work in. *Fig 60* shows three examples, but there are many more instances.

Even if the defenders play well, the men in possession have moves which may create space and opportunities to go forward. Here are some examples:
(a) A dribbles across the defender opposite him and at that moment B loops round behind A, receives a backward pass, and accelerates into the available space *(Fig 61)*. If the

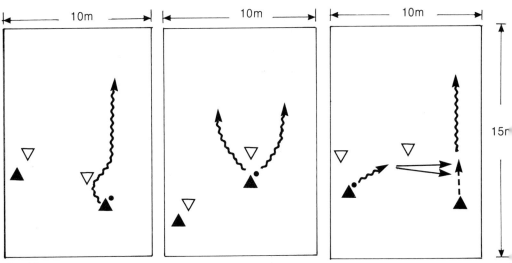

Fig 60

7. A and B are trying to combine by dribbling and passing to beat two defenders and take the ball over the end line. Here are some ideas to help:
(a) If the defenders are naïve enough to get themselves square, then a through pass and forward run may beat them *(Fig 59)*.

first defender looks to intercept, he has to step forward and A can dummy and go forward himself.

* How does A move to avoid being tackled?
* When does B move?
* When and where is the pass played?

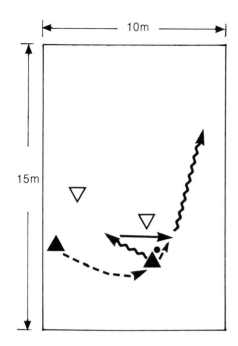

Fig 61

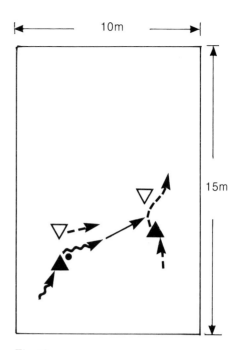

Fig 62

(b) A creates a passing opportunity to B by half beating his opponent while both attackers are moving forward *(Fig 62)*. As A opens up the reverse side of his opponent, the man marking B has to step slightly infield because a through ball would beat him. At that moment a pass onto B's stick will maintain the momentum of the move and give B an opportunity of beating his opponent.

(c) The same play can be set up by B initiating the move. This could happen when the man in possession is not in a position to get part of the way round his opponent. In this case B moves in towards the left shoulder of his opponent as he runs forward, but then swings out towards the right while at the same time partly turning to the left so that he can offer the stick to A as a target and see the pass coming

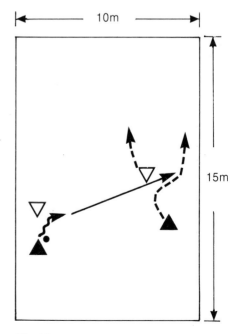

Fig 63

(Fig 63). The action of moving infield will also take the defender in and the swing outward then provides the space for the pass.

(d) The same ploys (b) and (c) can be modified for the left side of the field between, for example, CH and IL or IL and LW.

One further area needs practice before we can happily increase the stress on the attackers, and that is the effect on the forward pass of defenders who are closing players down.

Let us take a very simple example that we have already seen. If B's opponent leaves too much space behind or closes down too rapidly it is not difficult for A and B to combine to set up a telling through pass *(Fig 64)*.

However, let us look at a much more difficult situation for the man in possession, but one that regularly appears on the pitch particularly against Asian teams. In *Fig 65*, A has possession but his opponent is some distance away (say 10–12m). B is unmarked at present but A is a little uncertain about passing, for he thinks that the nearest opponent might anticipate and intercept the ball. The second defender is relying upon the hesitancy of A so that he can close in and mark B in such a way that he arrives at the same time as the ball *(Fig 66)*. We will find considerable advantages however, if A can make the pass as early as possible, so that B receives the ball before the defender can close him down. B then has the option of a return pass to A or moving on with the ball *(Fig 67)*. This kind of pass is best played early, especially if both players are moving forward, and gives the receiver every chance of setting up a successful subsequent move.

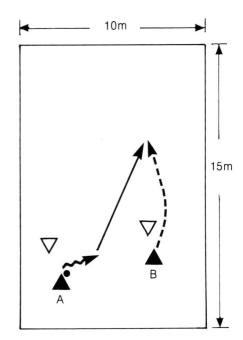

Fig 64

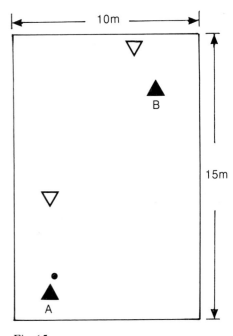

Fig 65

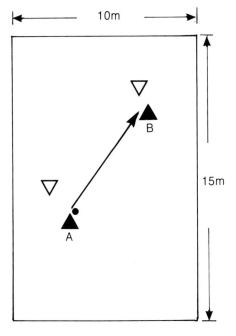

Fig 66

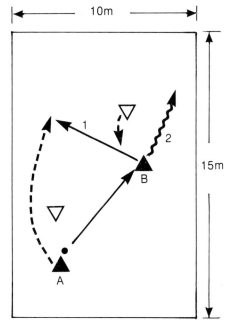

Fig 67

INCREASING STRESS

The coach should now be able to increase the stress on the attackers in a variety of ways as they have a sufficient repertoire of knowledge and skills. Here are some ideas:

1. Two attackers against a series of individual defenders who are not allowed outside their areas (Fig 68).
2. As in 1, but reduce the width of the areas.

3. As in 1, but reduce the depth of the areas.
4. As in 1, but make the areas larger and have three attackers against a series of defending pairs.
5. As in 1 but with the areas adjacent to each other. Three attackers aim to beat each of the defenders. The defenders cannot move out of their own area, but can help each other as much as possible.
6. Repeat 1 to 5, but at the end the attackers enter the circle and shoot at goal.

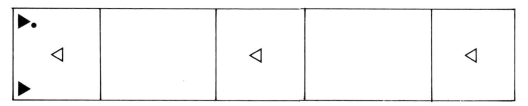

Fig 68

7. 3 v 2 in an area large enough to make defending difficult. The aim is for the three attackers to control the ball over the opponents' baseline.
8. As in 7, but 2 v 2.
9. As in 7, but 3 v 3.

CENTRING

Centring the ball is basically just another pass and so all the points considered in the sections on passing are also relevant here, but the one difference to all other passes is that a principal objective of a centre is to provide the receiver with every opportunity to score a goal. The emphasis, therefore, must be on giving the kind of pass the receiver requires in terms of pace, placement and timing.

No centre can be described as wrong if it is given to an attacking player, but there are areas of the circle in which either the defence is particularly vulnerable or an attacking player is likely to be able to receive a pass.

Right Wing Centres

1. *An early centre hit diagonally from the RW (Fig 69).* The aim of this centre is to play the ball goal-side of the defenders as they are running back to cover the fast break, for the CF to meet as he sprints forward. The shot is likely to be a controlled sweep with the forehand stick.

2. *An early centre hit square from the RW (Fig 70).* This situation can arise if the RW has looked to start a fast break round the outside of the LH but has suddenly stopped. The FBs or sweeper and CB have been retreating but stop immediately after the RW stops. If there is no defender (e.g. CH) between the RW and

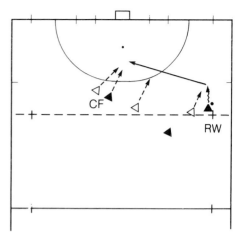

Fig 69

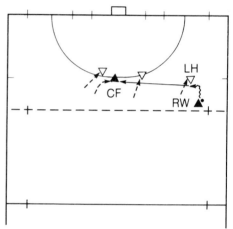

Fig 70

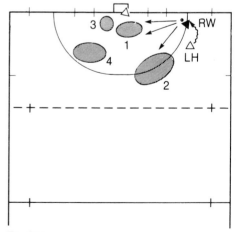

Fig 71

the CF, a hard flat centre to the forehand stick can give the CF an opportunity to get to the edge of the circle in a strong position.

3. *RW Centres from the baseline (Fig 71).* The RW has beaten or half beaten the LH and cut infield so that he is able to make all four passes. The CF (in area one) is looking to meet the ball about four to six metres out from the near post on his forehand stick. This may be a hit or a push/flick pass according to the situation and will be deflected at goal by the CF. The LW can be moving into area three near the far post to pick up a ball going in front of the CF.

The ball to the IR position (area two) is possible as the defence has been running back towards their goal. This is a difficult pass to hit accurately and needs skilful body positioning and work of the hands. The receiver aims to collect the ball outside the circle as this will give more time for the shot.

The fourth area is the least used and may appear to be blocked by defenders but sometimes the CH cannot stop this pass because he is pulled either towards the goal or the top of the circle. The LW can be on the line of the pass and often unattended because the RH has been drawn to protect the area in front of goal and has not seen the movement of the LW. This pass has to be hit very hard.

Left Wing Centres

Early centres from the LW usually take place after the LW has begun to go on the outside of the RH and then cut back to open up a pass from left to right *(Fig 72).*

According to the position of the defenders, the LW may hit the centre diagonally towards the far post to be met by the

CF or squarer to the CH or IR.

In *Fig 73* the LW has beaten the RH and cut in along the baseline, but it is difficult to hit the ball from here (unless the player is very good on his reverse stick hitting) because of the position of the ball and body and the proximity of defenders able to tackle with the forehand stick. Players therefore have to be able to push or flick the ball hard and accurately onto the forehand stick of colleagues

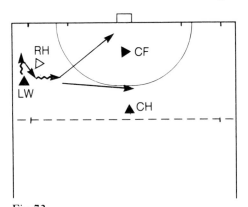

Fig 72

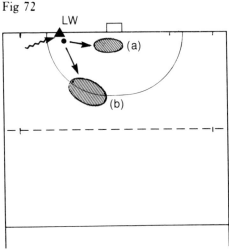

Fig 73

entering the two shaded areas. Deflections at goal are possible from zone (a), but on controlling the ball in zone (b) the player would have to reposition or pass the ball prior to shooting.

Practices

Build the practices up from a simple beginning. Here is one possible progression for all the centres:

1. Practise centres from the stationary position to players in the various areas.
2. As in 1, but the receivers move into position (and shoot) and have cones as defenders or obstacles for the passer to avoid.
3. As in 2, but the passers now move 5–10 metres before centring. It is important that the passer is well balanced as the centre is given.
4. As in 3, but have passive defenders.
5. Add more movements before the centre, for example wall pass with a colleague or receive a long pass and dribble.
6. Add more defenders/attackers as the coach desires.
7. Give the attackers a time limit in which to get into position, centre and shoot (semi-passive defenders).

SHOOTING

As with centring, shooting could be described as a pass into the goal, but the fact that a GK can use any part of his body to stop the shot necessitates that many shots are struck with venom.

The basic requirements for shooting are that the player is able to control the ball, position it and quickly manoeuvre the body so that a shot can be made as soon as possible. This requires strength, balance and co-ordination, but it is a learnt skill and players should go through progressive practices designed by the coach to develop this ability.

The following progressions are an example:

1. Stand one metre from the top of the circle (or any line) with the ball on the forehand stick, move forward with the ball and strike it at the goal (or target) before or as the ball crosses the line.
2. As in 1, but start with the ball to the left of the body.
3. Stand one metre outside the circle as in 1, but this time the player controls passes pushed from five metres away before moving forward and shooting. These passes should be given from the complete 360 degree range.
4. As in 3, but increase the distance of the passes.
5. Repeat practices 3 and 4, but stand inside the circle and control and shoot without moving forward.

Players should attempt to get into the best body position for every kind of shot so that even when they are off balance they maintain as good a technique as possible. Only by aspiring to a high standard of performance in practice will they acquire the good habits that will help them succeed in the game situation. In addition to having reliable shooting technique, players should also be able to hit, push, flick and deflect shots at goal from a variety of positions at various heights. Although players may be able to illustrate good technique and considerable skill in an unpressurised shooting practice, they need to be exposed to the difficulties of competition (marking) and space (congested areas).

Bearing in mind all the factors mentioned so far, coaches need to develop progressive practices to cover the following aspects of the skill of shooting:

1. Controlling a pass in or near the circle and then hitting, flicking or pushing at various heights at goal, with or without a GK.
2. Controlling a pass outside the circle, moving forward and then shooting as the ball crosses the line, with or without GK.
3. Dribbling from forty metres out and then cutting pace in order to prepare for various kinds of shot from the edge of the circle.
4. As in 3, but all shots must clear an obstacle resembling a sliding GK.
5. Dribbling around a semi-active defender before shooting against a GK.
6. Dribbling into the circle and shooting but being pressured by a defender chasing the player.
7. As in 6, but defender covering from the side.
8. Dribbling into the circle and trying to score against the GK coming out to meet the player.
9. Deflecting centres from LW and RW (*see* section on centring).
10. Introduce more competition, such as four attackers versus three defenders and a GK.
11. Practise controlling the rebounds from the GK and scoring with a variety of shots. The GK should deliberately play the first shot at the forwards so that they can practise.

No one can teach a player to have an appetite for scoring goals, but good practices will help develop sound technique, confidence in scoring, understanding between players, an instinct for where the goal is and an awareness of which shot to use at a particular time.

Outstanding goal scorers in open play capture the headlines but their danger is not innate, it is a combination of heredity, desire and hours and hours of practice!

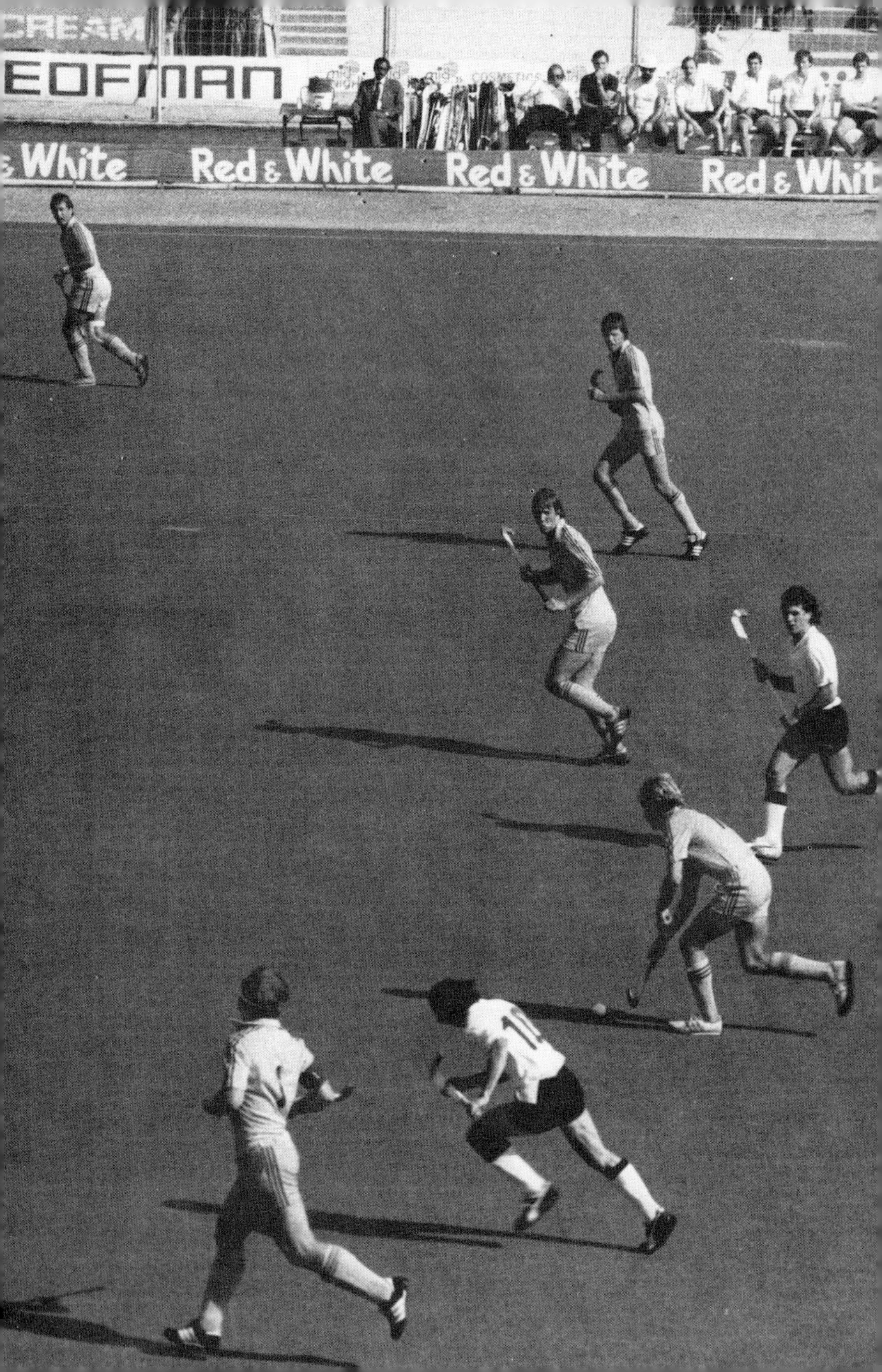

CREAM
EOFMAN
Red & White
Red & White
Red & White
Red & White

4 Promoting and Developing Off the Ball Skills

In Britain our hockey is too often character-ised by too much play and too little practice.

IN ATTACK

Support Play

In any passing sequence the movement of the attacking players without the ball can have a major influence upon the success of each pass. This section is concerned with this skill of supporting the man in possession.

The aim of all players in the attacking team should be to provide support by being available for a pass either directly from the man in possession or via a colleague. In the simple example in *Fig 75*, A has direct support from B and, while C is not offering a direct pass, the ball could get to C via B.

These supporting moves may be in a variety of forms. A supporting player may be:

* Close to the man in possession or some distance away.
* Stationary or moving.

* Moving in any one of a variety of directions.
* In front of, alongside or behind the man in possession.
* Moving quickly or slowly.
* Creating space for himself, or a colleague, or both.

The real skill of the players off the ball is to assess which movement will be most beneficial for the particular situation and, of course, the majority of situations are group skills and their success therefore depends very heavily upon several players moving in harmony.

A vital aspect of support play is an awareness of space and this must also be

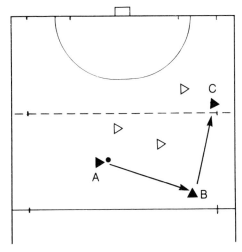

Fig 74 (left) Notice the support play for Australia and the desire of the West German No. 10 to get into the best position to defend.

Fig 75

seen from both an individual and group point of view. Players must understand how, when and where to move to get into the space most advantageous for their team. This will sometimes require players to move in such a way that creates space for a colleague rather than themselves. Awareness can only be achieved if players use their vision.

Look at *Fig 76*. In situation (a), the LH is breaking through with the ball close to the sideline, so the LW may move infield to take his marker away to provide space or, if the RH does not follow him, support in front of the ball. In situation (b), the RW would stay as wide as possible so that the two attackers had every chance of making use of the space infield and, if the LH moved in, the RW would be available for a pass.

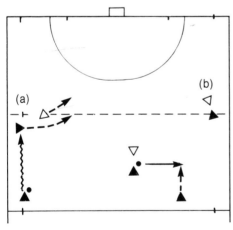

Fig 76

In order to achieve successful attacking moves, this understanding of support play must be combined with the skill of the man in possession to give the correct pass in terms of time, speed and direction.

Practices for supporting play are given in the section on practices for passing, but

it is relevant here to emphasise the principal coaching points.

1. Where is the space most advantageous to you or your team?
2. Can you use it or is it best for a colleague to move into it?
3. Do not fill the space too early if by doing so a defender will also be attracted, thus negating the advantage.
4. If your colleague is going to use the space, can you help by keeping other defenders away?
5. Can you offer the man in possession another pass, so increasing the defenders' problems?
6. Who initiates the move if you are to be the recipient of the ball?
7. What are the cues that you and/or the passer of the ball offer and look for?
8. Whether or not you are the recipient, what is your next move?

In a dynamic game such as hockey, the other major variable influencing support play is, of course, the movement of defenders. Players must be ready to respond to these changes without relinquishing the initiative and, again, ways of doing this are suggested in the advanced practices for passing.

IN DEFENCE

All defending skills are fundamentally off the ball skills, as gaining possession without the opposition scoring is the end product of good defensive work. When the opposition have the ball the principal aims of the defending team are to *delay any rapid attack* and *regain possession*. These aims are achieved by the use of a number of defensive skills: marking; covering;

Fig 77 Jim Irvine tries to get the stick in line with the likely
pass even though he is in a weak position. Notice
also the covering work of Trevor Smith, the centre half.
(West Germany v Australia, Champions Trophy 1982)

channelling or shadowing; closing down; and tackling. But underpinning all these skills is the art of any defender to position the body correctly, and throughout this section and the practices it must be kept uppermost in the mind.

Positioning

Questions that coaches and players should ask themselves during practice about their general positioning include:

* What are the opposition likely to do?
* What am I trying to achieve?
* What are the options of the man in possession?
* Can I limit these options?
* Am I contributing to effective defence?
* Can I regain possession?
* How is the situation changing and what is my response?

In defence, players initially respond completely to the position of the opposition *(delay any rapid attack)*, but as the defending team puts increasing pressure upon the man with the ball, the attacking options are reduced and the positions of the defenders can be reassessed and orientated more towards the aim of *regaining possession*. An example is given in *Fig 78*. As the LH gains possession, the opposing RH cannot afford to mark the LW too tightly as a quick pass to the IL could lead to an embarrassing through pass, but if the IR closes in on the LH and another defender approaches the IL, then the RH is able to quickly reassess the situation and mark more tightly.

It is important that coaches and players appreciate that all players have a defensive responsibility at various times in the game and must therefore understand all the defensive skills.

71

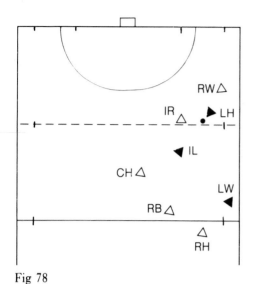

Fig 78

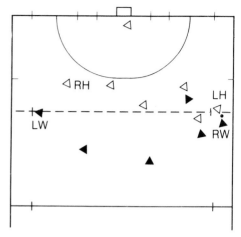

Fig 79

Marking *(Figs 79 & 80)*

This is a good starting point when learning defensive skills, as it is an easily understood concept and gives the defender a sound indication of where to position himself in relation to the ball, his opponent and his own goal.

Generally speaking, defenders position themselves on a line between their opponent and their own goal; their distance from the opponent will be influenced by the position of the ball and the need to consider covering other defenders. The greater the likelihood that the ball will be passed to their opponent, the closer the defender will be. When the ball is on the opposite side of the field, a wing half will be further away from his winger than when the ball is in the centre of the field *(Figs 79 & 80)*. There are, of course, exceptions to this ideal but more of that later.

The specific aims of marking are to deter any pass to the player or, if a pass is made, to intercept it or tackle the player as the ball arrives, or to harass the receiver so that an error is forced. In almost all situations the defender should be able to see the ball and the player being marked.

Most defenders (as opposed to midfield players and forwards) tend to mark directly behind or beside, but slightly backward of, the opponent, depending upon the line of the pass and the position of the attackers, but the position must always fit in with the overall aims of defending and the specific requirements of marking.

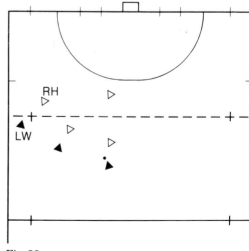

Fig 80

Practices for Marking

(Figs 81 to 84)

Small areas will facilitate all practices for defending.

1. *Marking an opponent when the pass is coming from behind (Fig 81).* The server passes (within five seconds) to his colleague who tries to control the ball and score by dribbling it over the end line and between the cones. The defender aims to inhibit the pass and tackle the man. The attacker should be reasonably passive at first so that the defender is successful.

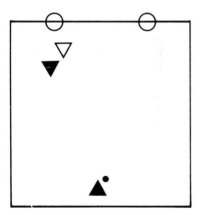

Fig 81

2. *Marking an opponent when the pass is coming from the defender's right (Fig 82).* The server passes so that the defender can practise intercepting on forehand and reverse stick. If the defender gets too close to the attacker a through pass should be given. Vary the practice by making the passes harder so that the interception is a little more difficult; making a longer pass towards the attacker; changing the angle slightly and repeating the practices.

Then extend the practice so that the forward now competes against the defender and tries to dribble the ball over the end line and between the cones.

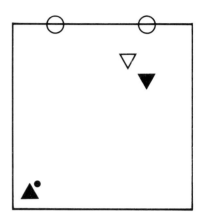

Fig 82

3. *Defending a pass from the left.* Repeat practices in 2, but defending a pass from the left *(Fig 83).*

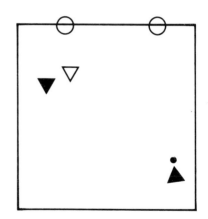

Fig 83

4. *Coping with the interchange of positions by attackers (Fig 84).* Attackers aim to receive the pass from the server and collectively beat defenders to score by dribbling the ball over the end line. The server cannot enter the area of play but he

can receive passes from the attackers. The attackers are encouraged to interchange positions.

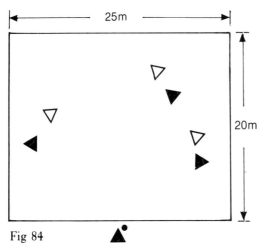

Fig 84

In midfield, exactly the same aims, objectives and techniques are used by the defending side but there are two very differing methods of implementing them. The first is man to man marking, where the midfield player takes the responsibility for marking behind or alongside his opponent and seeks to perhaps intercept the pass, but more often to tackle the man as he gains possession. The second method is to position the midfield player in such a way that intercepting the pass to the opposing midfield is the principal objective and in this case the marking is done alongside or in front of the opponent.

In reality, of course, the sophisticated team employs both methods. Marking in front of players depends very much upon the ability of several players to reduce the passing opportunities of the player on the ball and is, therefore, most effectively used at restarts or when the ball is pinned close to a sideline, whereas in a sudden counter-attack, when the defence is stretched and under pressure, a midfield player may have to mark his opponent very closely. More will be said about this in the section on team defence.

Covering *(Figs 85 to 87)*

The skill of covering in defence is to give defensive support behind the player immediately engaged in opposing the attacker in possession. This role is nearly always combined with that of marking a player and in almost every case it is important to achieve the correct balance between marking and covering. In situations where one of the nearest covering defenders has no marking responsibilities (for example a sweeper or disengaged full back), that man will become the engaged defender if his colleague ahead of him is beaten (this introduces the skill of channelling players). *Figs 85 to 87* show examples of covering.

Fig 85 With A1 in possession, D1 is the engaged defender. D2 and D3 are providing cover, but are also marking A2 and A3 respectively. D4 is a defender with-

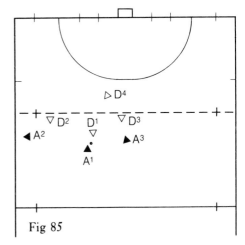

Fig 85

out any marking responsibilities covering the situation and, bearing this in mind, D4 could encourage D2 and D3 to mark their men more closely. If D4 were unable to cover as effectively, then D2 and D3 would have to offer more cover to D1. But the situation has to be dynamic to match the game.

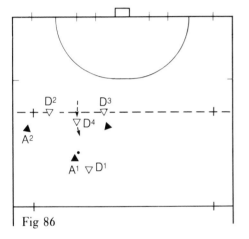

Fig 86

Fig 86 If D1 is beaten, then D4 as the player without any attacker to mark should now engage A1, while D2 and D3 provide the cover and marking balance.

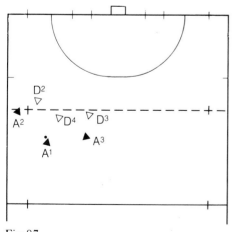

Fig 87

Fig 87 In this new situation of 3 v 3 and no free defender to cover, the defenders have to force the attackers away from the goal. In this case it is advantageous for the defence if D4 can push the attack towards A2. D2 can assist this by positioning himself so that the pass to A2 is attractive while D3 can mark A3 a little closer so threatening any pass towards A3.

Practice for covering is included in those for marking, channelling, shadowing and the group practices for defending.

Channelling and Shadowing Opponents

Channelling is a term usually applied to a situation where a player in possession of the ball is manoeuvred in such a way that he is forced to run into the tackling area of another defender. In the example of covering shown in *Fig 86*, A1 was channelled towards D4 through intelligent positioning and movement by D2 and D3.

Shadowing is a term applied to the skill of a defender to dictate the movement of the attacker in possession by clever body positioning. It is often used within the skill of closing a player down, as it also involves restricting the space and passing opportunities available to the attacker and moving the ball into a less dangerous area.

Practices for Channelling
(*Fig 88*)

1. The attackers score by dribbling the ball over the end line. The two marking defenders aim to channel the player in possession towards their own free defender, while making certain that they

75

provide cover as the player engages the attacker.

2. Begin as above, but the aim of the defenders is to force the ball to the LW and then channel that man down the flank to the covering defender.

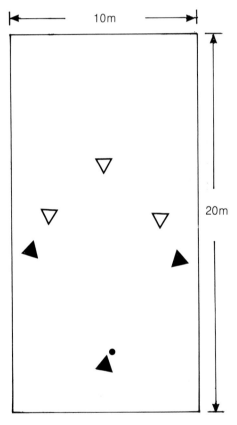

Fig 88

Practices for Shadowing
(Figs 89 & 90)

1. The aim of D1 is to engage the attacker and shadow the player towards D2 so that a tackle can be made *(Fig 89)*.
2. The attacker can vary his position so the defender has to shadow him to the

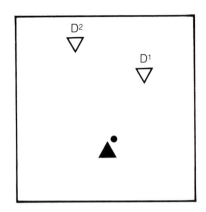

Fig 89

right or left, always towards his covering defender.

3. The attacker scores by dribbling the ball through the goal. The aim of the defender is to shadow the man to the side of the area further from the goal *(Fig 90)*
4. As in 3, but place the goal on the opposite side and shadow the man to the left. *Note*: The defender cannot leave as large an area on his reverse stick as he can on his forehand stick.
5. Repeat as in 3, but this time it is 3 v 2. The area can be larger to make it more difficult for the defenders.
6. 3 v 2. Repeat as in 5, but with the goal on the other side of the area.

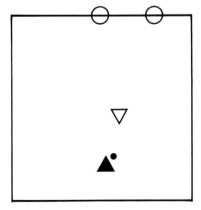

Fig 90

Closing Down

Closing down is when a defender approaches the man in possession. His aims are to:

1. Delay the forward movement of the player.
2. Restrict the passing opportunities available to the player.
3. Reduce the space and time the player has available.
4. Force an error or dispossess the player.
5. Give other defenders time to mark and cover, so increasing the pressure on the opposition.

Closing down begins before the particular opponent receives the ball and is inextricably bound up with the other defensive skills of marking, covering, shadowing, channelling and tackling. If one wanted to define it rigidly, closing down is the movement from a covering or attacking position to a marking position.

When practising closing down, players should ask themselves: How close shall I go? How close is my cover? Which way do I force the opponent? Can I get round so my forehand stick is in front of the player? Should I do so? Is the player moving forward? If so, how fast?

Closing down players and passes is one of the most important defensive skills for forwards. At restarts, especially free hits in the opposing half, the ability of forwards to close off gaps through which passes may be made upfield and close down defenders if a short pass is made is of great assistance to the rest of the defending team, as it allows the midfield players to look to intercept passes and the

half backs and full backs to mark and cover in the most effective way.

The aim of these forwards when closing down a defender should be to force the man in possession to move to the attacker's forehand stick. It is easier both to tackle and block the pass using this skill. If the defender can be forced to retreat, then that is also advantageous.

PRACTICES

Closing Down Players

STATIONARY PLAYERS (*Figs 91 & 92*)

1. The server passes to his colleague and the defender closes the player down and traps him in the corner (*Fig 91*). The player in possession beats the opponent or gains a free hit to win.
2. As in 1, but the defender attempts to trap the player in the left corner (*Fig 92*).
3. As in 1, but the defender forces the player into either the left or right corner.

MOVING PLAYERS

Repeat practices 1 to 3 above, but the defender cannot close down until the man in possession moves.

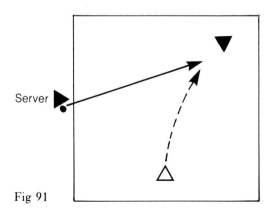

Fig 91

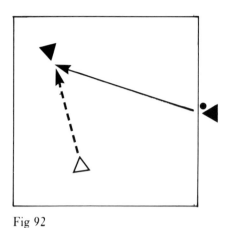

Fig 92

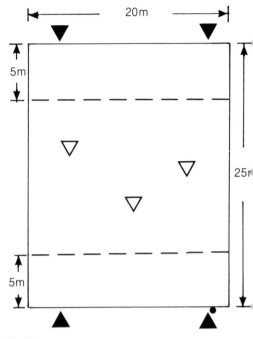

Fig 94

Closing Off Passes (Figs 93 & 94)

1. The aim of the players in possession is to pass the ball parallel to the sidelines to each other. (Fig 93). The defender experiments with how large a gap he can leave and still intercept the ball and how close he can go towards the man in possession and still make him hit the ball at the gap he is leaving on his open stick.
2. Repeat 1, but intercepting on the reverse stick.
3. The players in possession aim to pass

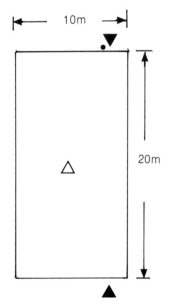

Fig 93

the ball on the floor across the area to their colleagues on the other side (Fig 94). They may pass the ball to their colleague on the same side of the area, but they cannot alter their positions. The defenders experiment to find the best way to stop the ball crossing the area, but they must stay in the central area.

Tackling

The ultimate aim of tackling is to win possession of the ball, but coaches and players must realise that it may only be possible to weaken the opponent's control over the ball or put the ball out of play in the tackle, thus giving the defending team time to reorganise.

The easiest tackles are those when the attacker is forced to:

1. Lose control of the ball as a result of pressure by the defender.
2. Move the ball to the defender's

advantage.

3. Make a poor pass which is intercepted or leads to a successful tackle by another defender.

While some players, because of their position, will primarily utilise one or two types of tackle, players ought to be able to perform all the tackles.

COACHING POINTS

The following general coaching points can be applied to all the tackles:

1. Watch the ball carefully and do not be confused by body and stick feints.
2. Keep the head of the stick near the ground and position the stick with thought. The player can then be encouraged to move the ball in a particular direction by clever stick positioning. Most players in possession will move the ball away from the defender's stick.
3. Use stick and body feints to pressurise the attacker in order to produce an error.
4. Do not run backwards as this is a weak position. If the attacker is running and has excellent control, then it is better for the defender to reposition the body and run alongside, but infield and slightly goalside of the attacker.
5. Good balance and nimble footwork are vital. Usually the defender has one foot in advance of the other as this allows swift movements in any direction.
6. Understand and, through intelligent body and stick position and movement, attempt to influence the alternatives available to the player in possession.
7. Defenders should not telegraph their intentions to the attacker, so the timing of the tackle is to the maximum advantage of the defender.

8. Tackling is easier if the attacker can be positioned on the defender's forehand stick.
9. Defenders should not rush into tackles when it is clear that the attacker has full control and can read the intentions of the defender.
10. A great deal of the preparatory work in tackling is done by the legs and these must be strong, as the defender is constantly working in the stooped position.
11. Defenders should work to dominate the attacker both physically and psychologically. In the latter area, the defender must aim to force the attacker to move in the least advantageous way.
12. Artificial turf pitches have allowed defenders to use a much more horizontal tackling technique in many situations.

Jab Tackle (Fig 95)

This tackle relies almost entirely upon the surprise element as it is not as strong as other tackles. The great advantage of the jab tackle is that the defender can surprise the opponent with the long reach he has as he steps forward and lunges with the stick in the left hand.

The stick must be held tightly in the left hand as this hand controls the stick, although the right hand can assist by

Fig 95 The jab tackle.

Fig 96 The Australian RW prepares to cut in around the goal-side of the Pakistan defender. Note the ball on the strong forehand side and the position of the defender in preparation for a jab tackle.

Fig 97 Trevor King makes an excellent low reverse stick tackle. Notice the distance he has had to reach and the tension in the left arm. (Australia v West Germany, Champions Trophy 1982)

throwing the head of the stick at the ball at the start of the tackle, and the grip is such that the palm of the hand and fingernails are facing upwards.

As the tackle is made the left foot steps forward, but it is important not to throw too much body weight over this foot, as this makes it very difficult to recover if a mistake is made. The stick jabs behind and under the ball forcing it beyond the attacker's stick and it is at that point that the defender steps further forward and returns two hands to the stick, if possible, in order to gain control of the ball. It is also possible to perform a dummy jab tackle and step back quickly to await the reaction of the attacker. The response to this kind of tackle is often to push the ball forward intending to put it close to the defender's feet and, by recoiling smartly, the latter can gain possession.

The jab tackle can be used to put the ball out of play when closing a wing player down from the side and may also be used by a player tackling back to jab the ball back towards colleagues.

Forehand Tackle

This tackle is probably the most commonly used and has to be performed close to the feet, wide on the forehand side, with the stick at various angles, and while the defender is stationary or running with an attacker.

The horizontal stick is particularly useful on artificial pitches as the ball runs smoothly and the stick can provide a more effective barrier, but in order to make use of this barrier the defender has to get closer to the ground which inhibits his ability to change position quickly.

The wide forehand tackle is often made possible by the defender closing down the attacker in such a way as to encourage the latter to move in the desired direction. All these tackles are usually begun with the left foot slightly in front of the right, as this enables the defender to change his position quickly and encourages the attacker onto the forehand tackle. It is not unusual to couple this tackle with a dummy jab tackle to the left of the ball to force the attacker onto the defender's forehand stick.

The situation often demands that a player makes a forehand tackle while running with an attacker. The defender positions himself so that he is able to run infield and ideally slightly goal-side of the attacker. The difficulty in this defensive skill is to make a timely tackle while running at speed and it is very important, therefore, to keep the attacker as wide as possible rather than be beaten.

Reverse Stick Tackle

This is a more difficult tackle to perform as it is dominated by the left hand (the weaker hand for most players), has to be made on players who primarily carry the ball to the right of their body and is influenced by the rules forbidding bodily or stick to stick contact during the tackle.

A clean reverse stick tackle is almost impossible to execute if the attacker is ahead of the defender and it is, therefore, imperative to be slightly goal-side. The skill is to trap the ball using the reverse stick, so that the attacker over-runs it or the ball can be played through the attacker and into a strong position for the defender. A second method of tackling on the reverse stick is using the horizontal tackle, but again it must be made level with or ahead of the defender's body if it is to be effective.

Whenever possible, it is advantageous to have two hands on the stick as it strengthens the tackle, but because one-handed tackles are common players with strong wrists and forearms have a clear advantage.

Practices for Tackling

The following practices are for the fore-hand tackles, but the basic formula can easily be adapted for the reverse tackles.

It is worth re-emphasising the following factors regarding tackling practices:

* Begin with a small area to provide success.
* In order to reinforce good technique, do not make it too competitive too early.
* Concentrate upon learning and practising the techniques at first.

FOREHAND TACKLE AGAINST
SLOW MOVING ATTACKERS
(*Figs 98 & 99*)

1. The attacker allows himself to be closed down and then tries to beat the defender on the forehand stick, but allows the defender to succeed (*Fig 98(a)*).
2. As in 1, but there is more space for the defender to cover (*Fig 98(b)*).
3. The server passes to his colleague and the defender closes down from a covering position and makes a forehand stick tackle (*Fig 99*). Change the angle of the pass and the position from which he closes down regularly.
4. Repeat practices 1 to 3, but now the attacker is encouraged to put the ball at the feet of the defender so that the defender practises the skill of taking the ball in this position.

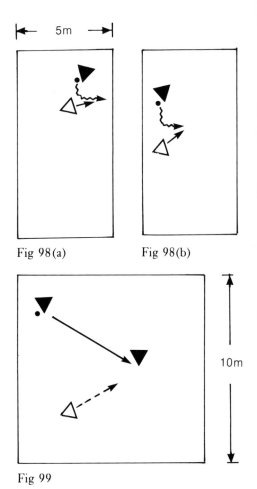

Fig 98(a)   Fig 98(b)

Fig 99

5. Repeat practices 1 to 4, but increase the width of the area to make the skill more difficult for the defender.
6. Increase the competitive nature of the practice.

FOREHAND TACKLES WHILE
RUNNING WITH ATTACKER
(*Figs 100 & 101*)

1. As the attacker runs with the ball, the defender positions himself correctly and tackles as the attacker momentarily loses control or takes the stick off the ball.

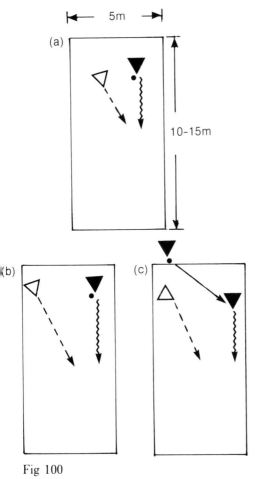

Fig 100

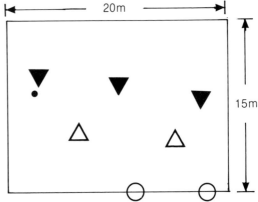

Fig 101   The attackers score by dribbling
the ball through the cones, while
the defenders score by making a
successful forehand stick tackle.

2. As in 1 but the defender has to make
up more ground across the area before a
tackle can be made.

3. The server passes to his colleague
moving forward and the defender has to
turn and then perform the skill of closing
down and tackling.

4. Repeat practices 1 to 3 but widen the
area.

5. Increase the competition but the
attacker must beat the defender through
the legs or on the forehand stick side.

6. A 3 v 2 situation in an area 15m by
20m. The three attackers score by dribbling the ball through the cones, while
the two defenders score by making a
successful forehand stick tackle.

Fig 102   Mark Precious (Great Britain) attacks West Germany's
circle while marked by Hannel. Note the level of
concentration.

5 Attacking Tactics in Open Play

Attackers may have flair but the vast majority of attacking play is made up of predetermined moves.

This chapter is concerned with linking together all the skills discussed in Chapter 3 with the basic principles which underpin attacking play, so as to achieve the objectives of the attack in hockey.

OBJECTIVES IN ATTACK

As in all games, the principal objective is to score more points or goals than the opposition. In hockey, goals are difficult to score because the ball must be touched by an attacker in the circle, which is only a small area of the pitch, and rules such as 'offside', 'dangerous play' and 'obstruction' restrict the freedom of individuals. The skills of possession, penetrating the defence and creating scoring chances should therefore be very important objectives in hockey at individual, group and team level. There is little wrong with individual attacks, but the major advantage of a group attack is that there is more support and, therefore, greater chance of a goal scoring opportunity.

Retaining possession of the ball is obviously a high priority when attacking, particularly during the early build-up in the defensive and midfield zones, but unless a team is able to penetrate the opposing defence causing defenders to turn and run towards their own goal, it is unlikely that many goal scoring opportunities will be created. (The longer a defence is able to delay any penetrative ploy by the attackers, the less space there will be to use and the more difficult it will be for the attacking team.) It will be seen that creating penetrative moves is, therefore, probably the principal vehicle leading to goal scoring chances.

PRINCIPLES OF ATTACKING TACTICS

The following principles must be considered during the planning of attacking moves aimed at penetrating the opposition defence and scoring goals:

* Width.
* Support.
* Mobility and understanding.
* Assessment and improvisation.

Width *(Figs 103 to 106)*

Width is the space between attackers across the pitch and this must be studied intelligently if it is to be used to the advantage of the attacking side (conversely, unintelligent use can help the defence).

Functioning with as much width as is feasible can produce advantages such as:

1. More space for each attacker to work in.
2. It stretches the defence and makes covering and closing down harder work.
3. It creates gaps in the defence that may be exploited by through passes or players running with the ball.

(Fig 103) Width in this situation is important as the defenders have to decide where to leave themselves exposed. The defenders have sensibly concentrated their forces in the most dangerous area, leaving the LW free. However, good use of the LW by the attackers could still cause the defence problems.

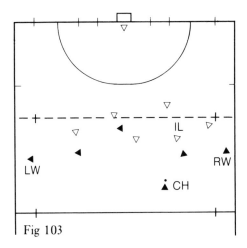

Fig 103

In some cases it is advantageous to alter the spacing between players across the field. In the situation in *Fig 104* the forwards have moved away from the RW leaving a possible 1 v 1 situation in a large area of the field.

In *Fig 105*, even the RW has moved infield to leave a space to be exploited by a defender coming forward.

In these cases the ball has gone to a player providing width to the attacking team, but it is also possible for players to

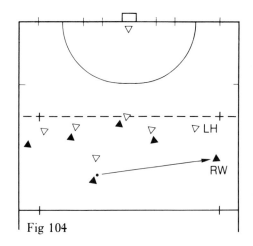

Fig 104

deliberately reduce the width in order to use it when they have gained possession.

Look at *Fig 105*, but instead of the pass going to the RH, imagine it goes to the RW coming back into space. Once in possession the RW has considerable space outside the LH to utilise, particularly if the RW has pace.

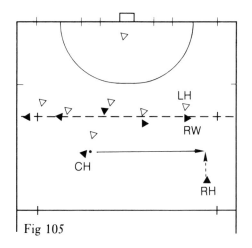

Fig 105

Finally it is important to realise that to use width advantageously the attackers must understand the emphasis that defenders will place upon the width they offer to the opposition. As a team approaches the attacking circle, the defenders will close ranks to protect the shooting area, reducing the width that is most advantageous to the attackers. It is vital that any attacker's position in the last 25 m of the pitch provides both width to the attack and an immediate threat to the defence.

Look at *Fig 106*. The position of the LW1 does not worry the RH unduly as there may be far greater danger points near the circle. But if the LW moves to LW2 the RH has to pay far more attention, as the LW is now still giving sufficient width, but more importantly has become a greater threat to the shooting area. It is a difficult concept, but for forwards the widest position is not always the best position.

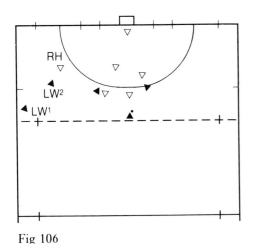

Fig 106

Support

Support play has been discussed already in Chapter 4, but it is vital that in attack there is support behind, beside and in front of the ball if penetration is to be achieved. Good support play will provide the team with several possible solu-

tions to the problem of penetrating the defence and it is important that players are able to respond to changing circumstances. It is not unusual for the defence to read and threaten 'Plan A', and if the attacking players cannot maintain the pressure on the defence, they are unlikely to be successful. The ability to overcome this kind of problem is dependent upon players being able to put into action all the concepts and skills illustrated in this chapter.

Mobility

Mobility, that is being able to change position without any detrimental effect upon the team, is not merely a useful attribute but an essential skill, especially for forwards as it may make the difference between unpicking a defensive unit and a stalemate situation. Players should not only appreciate the role of positions they might find themselves playing in, but also actively experience them.

Understanding

Understanding between players is important in all aspects of team play and comes from hours of practice. It is vital that players do not always work with the same person, but it is also very advantageous for players who play close together in the game to know each other's play well.

Players must be encouraged to talk to each other during practice so that small but significant areas of possible error are ironed out. For example: Where do they want the ball passed to? When do they move? When do they pass the ball? How hard should the pass be? and so on.

The second part of understanding –

Fig 107 Richard Dodds looks for the best pass as he approaches
the attacking 25, while Martyn Grimley offers support
ahead of the ball and performs a neat piece of
obstruction! (Great Britain v Pakistan, Perth 1985)

knowing what the player is going to do – is a result of practising patterns of play in a wide variety of circumstances, but more of that later in the chapter.

Assessment and Improvisation

These are integral aspects of attacking play but again they must work within the patterns of play previously mentioned. Every player must assess the attacking situation as it develops, so that the timing, direction and pace of any movement of ball and/or body is in harmony with the rest of the players. As the understanding of each other's play and the patterns of play increase, so the ability of two or more attackers to identically assess a situation and respond accordingly also increases. This is the key to patterns of play and therefore team play.

Within this framework, improvisation must be allowed and in fact demanded because there are bound to be instances when wrong decisions are made and players consequently face an unexpected problem. Encourage players to improvise, but demand that the improvisation fits with the team requirements and is not made at the expense of a much more beneficial and easily executed move. Players *must* be confident to make decisions on the field, but they must also be ready to justify them to their colleagues – and their coach! This improvisation may, of course, be on or off the ball, for example changing position in order to support an attack.

There is a second aspect of assessment which is fundamental to any attacking strategy and that is the assessment of the team's attacking qualities. This is, of course, a continuous process as improved skills and understanding coupled with meaningful practice will further develop attacking qualities. However, I would suggest a rather more simplistic but nonetheless important starting point. For example:

* Have the forwards got genuine pace? This will affect the exploitation of the space behind the defenders.
* Is there a player who has the ability to score goals?
* Have the inside forwards/midfield the vision to release the forwards?
* Have the forwards the skill to beat a man at pace and/or in congested areas?

Realistic assessment will provide both a starting point and a pointer to attacking tactics likely to produce success.

PENETRATIVE (INCISIVE) MOVES

Penetration of the opposition's defence is created by putting the ball and a player into a space behind or goal-side of a defender. This is achieved by a combination of dribbling, passing and supporting. All these skills along with the concept of making space have been described, but to complete the picture the attackers must be clear in their minds which spaces they are trying to exploit at any one time. There is always some space available to the attackers but its size, location and accessibility and the length of time it is available are constantly changing. It is worth assuming as an attacker that good defenders rarely leave large and dangerous spaces behind or

goal-side of them that are easily accessible. When these spaces do occur the defence will not let the attack exploit them without the latter having to work very hard. The difficulty in scoring goals confirms this.

So where are the spaces? *Fig 108* illustrates both the spaces available and the problems of exploiting them when the IR is in possession. Space 1 can be utilised by the RW but this is not a direct penetrative pass and the LH would be happier to see this used than a more dangerous space behind him.

Space 2 can be utilised by the CF and this is a penetrative pass but the positioning of the IL, LB and LH make the space small. Space 3 is larger and potentially more dangerous, but the defenders will position themselves so that it is difficult to get both ball and attacker successfully into the space.

Spaces 4 and 5 are dangerous but again the position of the defenders restricts rapid exploitation of these areas. Space 6 is the largest area but the most difficult to exploit with a direct pass. Consider how this situation changes if the defending IL or IR is not there or one of the defenders changes position.

Coaches should locate the spaces that could be available during any attacking move and assess how they can be exploited, by whom, and what alternative patterns should be used according to the response of the defence. The fact that there is never just one solution to the problem of creating penetrative moves indicates that players must go through a decision making process when considering the exploitation of a particular space. This decision making may well follow the lines shown in *Fig 109*.

Throughout the process, attacking

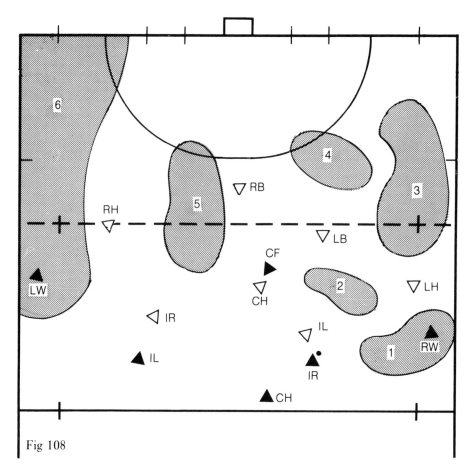

Fig 108

players are reassessing the situation according to the movement of the defenders, and the art of successful team play is the corporate recognition of the best alternative and its execution. These alternatives are the patterns of play that a team must develop so that understanding between players can be refined to the point where team play functions smoothly but not necessarily in an easily predicted way and so that even when the play is predictable, it is performed with such precision that the chances of success are very high.

The raw materials available to a team to develop attacking tactics are the skills of passing, controlling, dribbling, support play, interchanging positions and utilising space. However, it is not sufficient just to have these skills, no matter how abundant they may be in a team. They have to be organised so that the players are able to create attacking tactics (penetrative moves) in a variety of situations including:

1. When they have or can create numerical superiority, for example 4 v 3, 3 v 2 or 2 v 1.
2. When they are faced with numerical equality, for example 2 v 2 or 1 v 1.
3. When there is support ahead of the ball.
4. When there is support behind the ball.
5. When the area best used is congested.
6. When the area best used is away from the congested zone.

Before a coach can begin to develop these attacking tactics in the game situation, the players must be capable of performing all the passing, running, dribbling and controlling skills that will be asked of them and these are best practised in pairs and threes away from the game. It would be impossible to illustrate all the attacking tactics that could be developed, so I have given a few from each category listed above.

ATTACKING TACTICS

Numerical Superiority
(Figs 110 to 112)

It must be remembered that these situations rarely last for very long and it is imperative that the attackers recognise the situation immediately and react accordingly. The objective is to create a situation where there is ideally a 2 v 1 or at worst a 1 v 1 position.

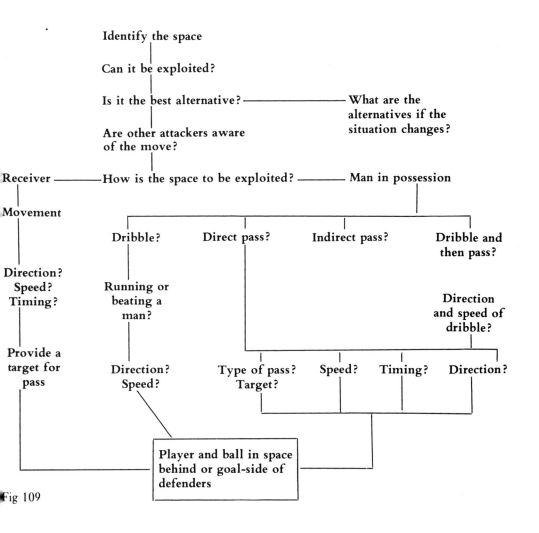

Fig 109

5 V 4, 4 V 3 AND 3 V 2 (*Fig 110*)

The situation shown in *Fig 110* illustrates all three examples as in the game
situation this is often how it proceeds or
should proceed. No matter which of the
forwards has possession they must attempt to make capital of the situation
before another defender, in this case the
CH, can recover and equalise the sides. If
the ball starts on either wing, the player
in possession must quickly assess whether
the space behind the WH can be exploited
by a 1 v 1 or a 2 v 1 using the IF. Undue
delay will allow not only the CH to
retreat and the FBs to mark but also the
opposite WH to come infield and pressurise the attackers, leaving the other
winger, the least dangerous forward, out
wide. An early pass to the IF could lead
to the possibility of further combination
play between the IF, CF and W or the
two IFs and the CF against two defenders. In this situation, therefore, it is vital
that the winger passes or penetrates early
in order to exploit the space behind the
defenders.

If one of the inside trio has the ball then
a quick pass to the CF would set up a 3 v
with the centre man in possession. Thi
man only has to run at either of the FBs t
create a 2 v 1 with the IF.

A CLOSE LOOK AT 2 V 1 (*Figs 111 & 112*

In *Fig 111* the support is ahead of the RW
and the space to exploit is behind the LH
so an early pass to the IR will give both
attackers time to set up the return and th
penetration.

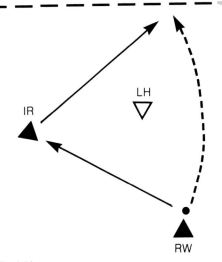

Fig 111

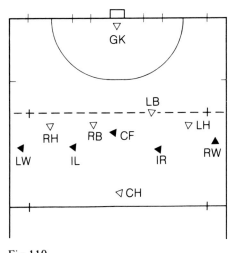

Fig 110

In the situation in *Fig 112* the long
defender is positioning himself between
the attackers in the hope that he can slow
their progress by threatening the interception as well as the tackle. The forward
must not hesitate to act: an early pass wil
force a reaction from the defender and i
he moves across, the return pass is open
moving towards the defender, particularly if he is retreating, will force a response

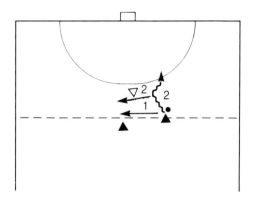

Fig 112

and then a pass or a dummy will produce the penetration.

Although it is possible to play 2 v 1 in an infinite number of ways, there are distinct advantages to the attackers if they aim to play the ball from left to right when beating the defender. The advantages include:

1. The passes are given and received with the forehand stick.
2. The pass can be played across the weaker reverse stick of the defender.
3. Intercepting by the defender is more difficult.
4. The receiver is able to go forward in a strong position with the ball on the forehand stick or play a wall pass.
5. The passer can use deception in this strong position to give a late pass or beat the defender before passing.

Numerical Equality

These situations are far more common and the objective is to create a 2 v 1 or a position where the receiver of the pass has a positional advantage over his opponent.

RIGHT WING AND INSIDE RIGHT
(*Figs 113 to 115*)

Fig 113 If the RW and IR can collect the ball and run at defenders as a pair then a square and through pass performed at reasonable pace can produce penetration. Notice the line of run and the angle of the passes.

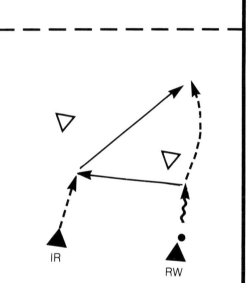

Fig 113

In *Fig 114* the IR has moved diagonally with the ball towards the RW and LH. If the LH stays close to the RW then the space behind the LH can be exploited.

Fig 115 In this situation both IR and RW may be moving forward. As the IR opens up the reverse side of his opponent, the LH has to be wary of the through pass and steps infield. He is encouraged to do this by a slight infield run by the RW. The RW steps out towards the sideline

93

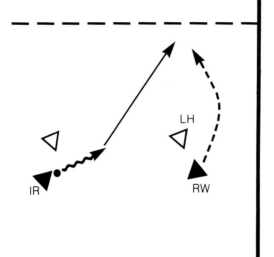

Fig 114

and the IR passes the ball firmly to his forehand stick. This puts the RW level with the LH and he should be able to exploit the space behind him.

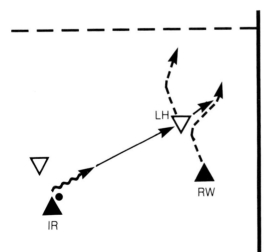

Fig 115

INSIDE FORWARD AND CENTRE FORWARD *(Fig 116)*

It may be possible to play a square and through pass in the situation in *Fig 116* but because IL and CF are often performing this 2 v 2 close to the circle, the latter part of the move is threatened by the GK. Another possibility, therefore, could be this: the IL shaping to go to the left, changes direction and drives at the LB. At the moment the IL changes direction, the CF moves to his right. The aim is to cause the LB to hesitate and although it may only happen for a fraction of a second, it is then that the pass is made to the CF. As the FBs need not offer any great depth in this situation, the pass must be right at the target to avoid interception.

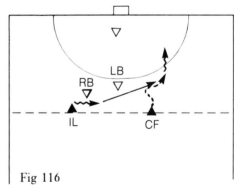

Fig 116

INSIDE LEFT AND LEFT WING *(Figs 117 & 118)*

The IL may run forward as a pass comes from behind and leave it for the LW *(Fig 117)*. The IL then continues in an arc to offer a through pass to the LW. If the RH does not cut off the channel it can be played, but if he does the LW can cut infield utilising the space left by the IL. Alternatively, the IL receives the pass

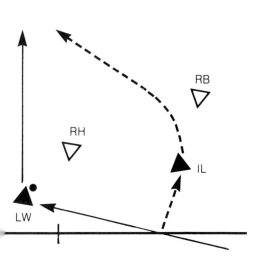

Fig 117

whether or not he steps infield to cut out the through ball. The indecision gives the LW and IL the time to set up either of the passes. If the LW stays wide, then both passes are possible but if he cuts in too early the job for the RH is much easier.

Support Ahead of the Ball

If a long crossfield pass (20m or more) is required before the through ball, then make it a hard pass as this gives the defence less time to plug the gap. The smaller or more distant the gap through which the penetrative pass has to be made, then the harder the ball must go. If the pass cannot be perfect, then err on the side of giving it too early or too hard as this is less likely to result in an interception.

INSIDE RIGHT AND CENTRE FORWARD (Fig 119)

As the IR opens up the reverse stick side of his opponent, a forward pass to the CF running left to right allows possession to be retained behind the opponents' half back line and in a position where the CF can exploit the defender's reverse stick side. A similar pass can be given to the CF from RH.

INSIDE LEFT AND CENTRE FORWARD (Fig 120)

Few CFs enjoy collecting through passes on the left-hand side of the field in the attacking third, as they can be channelled further left too easily, but a hard pass right onto their sticks in the centre of the field can give them an opportunity to go right or left. It is not an easy pass to give or receive, but one worth investigation.

nd drifts left and slightly forward with he ball (Fig 118). His opponent is often oncerned that he will cut back to the ght very suddenly and so lets him run ft. The RH now has a problem as to

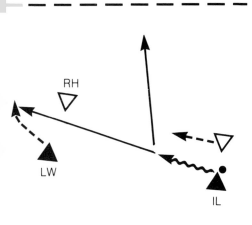

Fig 118

95

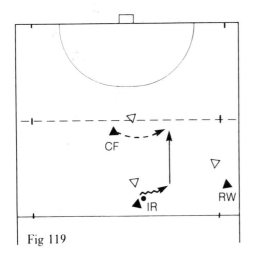

Fig 119

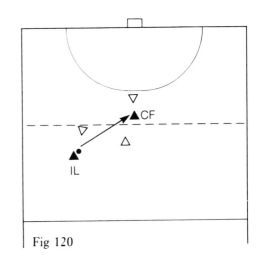

Fig 120

RIGHT HALF AND RIGHT WING
(Fig 121)

One of the most difficult situations is to pass from RH to RW when the RH is close to the sideline. The simplest but rarely used move is for the RW to come infield and then offer a pass onto his reverse stick or even better into the space behind the LH. The second ploy is best used against man to man markers.

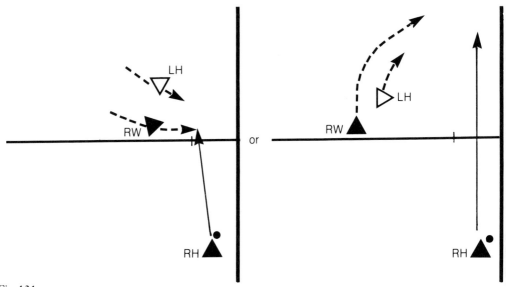

Fig 121

Support Behind the Ball

Penetration in this situation is gained by a man running from behind the ball and either gaining possession in front of or behind the defence. The space exploited by the player running from a deep position can be close to the point of possession or some distance from it and the type of pass can also vary considerably.

RIGHT HALF IN ATTACK
(Figs 122 to 124)

The RW has to hold the ball long enough to draw the LH infield and allow the RH to drive forward. If the pass cannot be given square to the RH there is no reason why the move cannot be completed via the IR *(Fig 122)*

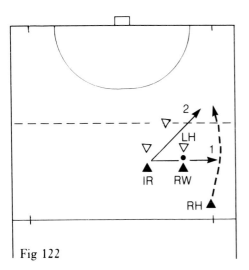

Fig 122

To make an incision well away from the ball, the defence has to be manipulated by the forwards and then a hard crossfield pass made so that the RH driving forward can take the ball and get beyond the

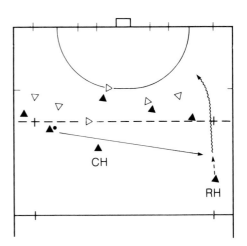

Fig 123

defenders as quickly as possible *(Fig 123)*.

In *Fig 124* the defence is kept reasonably open by the IR remaining level or behind the ball, the RW staying wide and the CF drifting left. Because the ball is likely to have to go close to one or two defenders the pass will have to be hit very hard and disguised. The timing of the move is crucial and if the RW becomes too isolated the LH will automatically cut infield to protect the danger point.

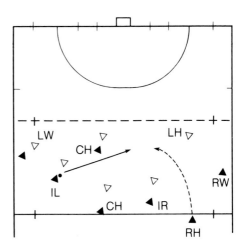

Fig 124

A Congested Area

Congestion must not deter players from making penetrative moves although the congestion puts certain extra constraints upon the participants. These constraints are obvious to any coach but they necessitate even more practice to perfect the moves.

Congestion requires that:

1. The passes are very accurate and usually need to be directly on the stick and made firmly.
2. The position of the receiver of any pass is taken up intelligently, thus maximising the chances of success.
3. Deception is used to confuse the defenders.
4. The players move quickly but with poise and control.
5. The ball is collected as safely as possible without obstructing the defender.
6. The timing of the move is immaculate.
7. The receiver controls the ball and immediately develops another movement (for example pass, dribble or shoot).

An Uncongested Area

(Figs 125 & 126)

Although players realise that it is best to attack an uncongested space, this is often difficult to achieve. Two examples have been given in the section on attacking with support behind the ball, but all too often it requires a crossfield pass prior to the incisive pass and because this takes time the defence has an opportunity to plug the gaps. Here are two very different examples, the first *(Fig 125)* a through pass to the RW after a crossfield pass and the second *(Fig 126)* an aeriel pass into space.

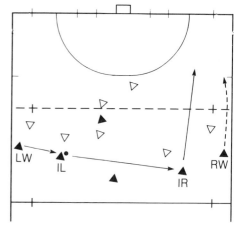

Fig 125

In *Fig 125* the ball has been switched quickly from the left flank to the IR. As the IR controls the ball, the RW sets off up the wing as fast as possible, keeping as wide as he can. The IR plays the ball through the gap which will be narrowing rapidly as the LB and LH move to close it. The ball can, and should, be passed at pace as the RW is travelling quickly.

Fig 126 illustrates the use of an aerial pass into a less congested area. This pass is one of the most difficult in hockey

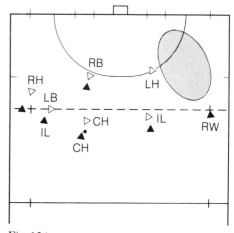

Fig 126

Fig 127   Great Britain's Martyn Grimley rounds the Pakistan left
half, while Robert Clift rests in the background.

(particularly the chipped hit) but its intelligent use can open up the game in an exciting way. The major difficulty in using the aerial pass (flick) is that it is not easy to disguise and the players must realise that the defenders are likely to read the intention. It is therefore imperative that the receiver anticipates the pass, as it must be played so that the defenders find it almost impossible to stop.

If the play has been concentrated on the left side for some time, defenders can be drawn across but still provide a solid barrier to crossfield passes. In this situation an aerial flick from IL, LH or CH into the area beyond the LH or, if he is still wide, in front of him can put considerable pressure on the defence.

There are many other situations when the aerial pass is useful, particularly when playing a pass into space behind the defenders for the forwards to exploit. On artificial turf these passes have to be judged very carefully as the ball races away if the trajectory is too low. The examples given are only some of the possibilities and coaches are encouraged to work with their players to discover more solutions to the problem and which best suit their particular style of play. It is also important to recognise which moves are best used against man to man defence and which against zonal marking, or perhaps it doesn't matter!

From the Back

Before leaving this chapter it is necessary to consider the role of defenders in attacking play. Although all defenders will provide support to the attack by moving upfield and offering players ahead of them backward and crossfield passes, greater responsibility than simply that is invested in defenders. Most attacks start with the ball in the possession of one of the defenders (half backs and full backs) and so they make the first attacking pass. Tactics at set pieces are covered later, so I will assume that the ball has been intercepted or won in a tackle. Defenders and coaches must consider the following factors related to the distribution of the ball in open play:

1. Pass early and quickly away from the point of tackle to reduce the chance of the attacker regaining possession.
2. Always look to pass forward as soon as possible. Go sideways to create a forward pass.
3. If a pass has been intercepted, the defender should pass and support the receiver to counter-attack the opposition.
4. Generally speaking, there are more passing opportunities and greater problems for the opposition to intercept passes when the ball is distributed from the central area of the pitch (FB and CH).
5. Wing halves can be very useful distribution points, but they can also be restrictive if the opposition can close the area down efficiently. Unless there is a large amount of space available to a wing half it

Fig 128   A good example by the Australian player of looking for a pass while moving forward in a strong position.
(Australia v New Zealand, Los Angeles 1984)

is best to give him the ball when he is able to move forward, as this makes him far more difficult to close down. RH is an easy position in which to receive the ball, but one of the most difficult to distribute from as almost all passes are across the forehand stick of the opposition.

6. Passes straight up the field (parallel to the sidelines) are difficult to collect in the midfield because of the problems of obstruction and the increased opportunity for the markers to tackle the man in possession in this congested area. For these reasons most passes to the midfield area are angled.

7. Passes straight upfield are used, but many are longer and aimed at the CF or to a midfield player in plenty of space.

8. Consider how man to man marking will influence the role of defenders in attacking play when they intercept or dispossess an opponent.

9. WHs are often used to support the midfield and of these the RH is usually the more attacking. Not only can they work closely with their IF, CH and W, but they often provide the team with a target for a long hard crossfield ball to switch the point of attack.

10. The CH is a major link in the centre of the field between defence and attack. In open play the CH must give support to the flank on which the ball is located, not only to help maintain the attack but also to provide the pivot through which the ball can be transferred to the other side of the field.

Attacking is a team skill in which all participate even if the principal role of a defender is to give the first pass of the attack and provide the necessary balance, cover or support to the move.

'Goal scorers may get the glory but the team gets the credit.'

'Too often attackers wait for something to happen so that they can implement a move. It is much more positive and effective if the attacking side makes it happen!'

Fig 129   An Indian forward is isolated by Australian players.
Notice that all three defenders have their sticks near the
floor. (Ric Charlesworth - IR; Peter Hazelhurst - IL;
Trevor Smith - CH.)

6 Defensive Tactics in Open Play

Defending, like attacking, is a group skill.

It must be pointed out that for a more complete picture of defending, this chapter must be combined with the defence of set pieces (Chapter 7).

OBJECTIVES IN DEFENCE

Having considered attacking tactics it is not difficult to flip the coin over and find that the main objectives in defence are:

* To stop penetrative passes.
* To reduce the goal scoring opportunities to a minimum.
* To regain possession and begin an attack.
* To defend effectively as far up the field as possible.

The art of defending is to develop both the individual and group skills to such a level that the opposition find it hard not only to exploit space behind or goal-side of defenders but also to make maximum capital of the situation even when it does occur.

DEFENSIVE REQUIREMENTS

The skills of closing down, channelling, tackling, marking, covering and inter-cepting have all been covered in a previous chapter; the importance of these in group defence will be illustrated by the examples later in this chapter. The only way a coach can develop the understanding imperative in group defence is to expose the group to the problems that they will face and demand that they assess their solutions and the alternatives that are available at any one time. Players must be ready to be decisive when defending but not rash, as the critical decisions usually occur in the most dangerous defensive zone, around and inside the circle.

Other attributes, such as calmness under pressure and a high level of concentration, often differentiate excellent defenders from very good ones.

There are, however, two more areas of knowledge that are prerequisites for a high quality defender: an understanding of the alternatives available to the attack and the most advantageous position to take up against them. These areas come under the vague term of 'reading the game', but their importance should not be overlooked by a coach as they usually mean the difference between 'a group of individuals defending' and 'group defence'.

Only when players have both the skills and the knowledge do they begin to develop the communication which cements the unit together. Calls should be clear, concise and informative so that the

	COSTS		BENEFITS	
ZONAL	1	Some players mark in front of their opponents and therefore cannot see both ball and man.	1	The ball can be kept in an area by intelligent positioning.
	2	A zone may be overloaded by the opposition creating a 2 v 1.	2	Intercepting leads to counter-attacks.
	3	Understanding of positional play, cover, closing down etc. is of paramount importance.	3	Defenders learn to cope with an extra man, thus allowing a more attacking philosophy.
	4	Intercepting passes is risky.	4	Defending is less physically demanding.
MAN TO MAN	1	A weak link can expose the whole team.	1	The roles are simple.
	2	Defender can be deliberately moved to certain areas by the opposition.	2	It is difficult to escape the marking and utilise any available space.

Fig 130

receiver can take immediate action, if necessary. The players behind or on the opposite side of the field to the play are often in the best position to call, as is the GK in many defensive situations.

Finally, defence is an ever changing situation demanding continual reassessment and action. All defenders must be alert at all times.

Man to Man and Zonal Defence

I do not intend to enter a debate over which system is the most effective. I merely put forward a kind of crude cost/benefit analysis. Coaches must assess their team and develop their defensive tactics accordingly. To draw up the table in *Fig 130* I have to assume that the defence marks exclusively either zonally or man to man. In reality, all teams utilise both types of defence, but it is important for a coach to establish the system on

which the team will base its defence.

The following sections relate to the 5-3-2-1 playing formation as used by England and Great Britain since 1983. Defence is based upon zonal marking, but it will be clear that it varies according to the situation.

DEFENSIVE COMBINATIONS

In this section the defensive priorities and responsibilities of certain combinations of players will be outlined with the help of examples. In the game situation all these combinations have to work in harmony and so it is imperative that players firstly practise the skills and secondly know the objectives of their colleagues. Both these responsibilities are firmly invested in the role of the coach.

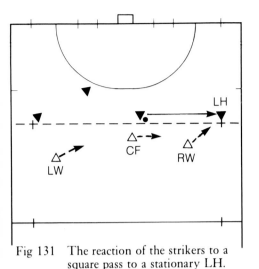

Fig 131   The reaction of the strikers to a square pass to a stationary LH.

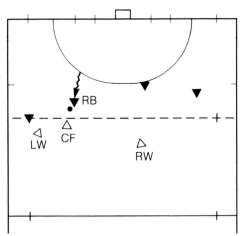

Fig 132   The RB advances with the ball, but the CF restricts his passes forward and the wingers make it as difficult as possible for the WHs to be brought into play in an effective manner.

Centre Forward and Wings

(Figs 131 to 133)

INDIVIDUALLY

1. Pressurise opponent when he has possession, restricting his passes.
2. Tackle back immediately, if tackled.
3. Harass a defender breaking away with the ball.
4. Cover a dangerous move off the ball by a defender.
5. Listen for and react to calls from colleagues on defensive positioning.

GROUP

1. Force passes to go out wide.
2. Encourage a pass to a stationary WH and close the player down rapidly using winger and CF with the opposite wing coming well infield.
3. Help the midfield by threatening passes to IF areas.

Inside Forward and Centre Half Combination

When the ball is nearer the opposition's goal, the IFs position themselves to either

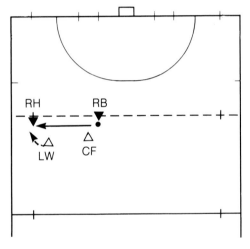

Fig 133   The RB has passed to the RH, but the LW has closed down the latter very effectively.

cut out the pass to the IF or mark alongside and infield of the player so that an interception or tackle can be made. The CH will be between the ball and his own goal and slightly infield of the ball *(Fig 134)*.

The CH will only become involved if the ball reaches an IF in the clear and he is

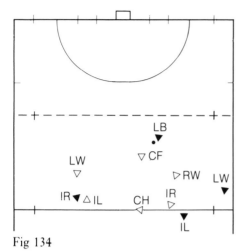

Fig 134

close *(Fig 135)*. In this case he will have to decide whether to tackle or push the player wide or channel his run into the FB. In this situation the defending IF on the opposite side must try and get between the ball and the IR to stop the pass square. The LH, seeing the danger, will move infield to provide cover as the FBs react to the situation.

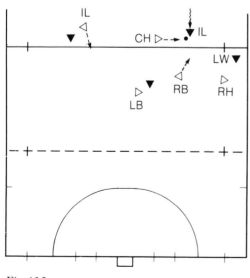

Fig 135

Centre Half and Full Back Combination

The combination within this group has just been illustrated *(Fig 135)* and the defensive role of the CH is therefore rather difficult to explain. He stops any pass put down the middle of the field in as wide a channel as possible. He closes down any player breaking through the midfield in his area *(see example above)*, but he must be a master of delaying tactics so that reactions to his movement can be made by others alongside and behind him. As the trio of FBs and CH get nearer their own circle, the CH must dominate the area near the top of the circle, forcing the opposition wider. The positional play of the CH is vital as defenders will often take up their defensive positions in relation to the CH.

Full Backs

Along with the LH, the full backs theoretically have the most defensively orientated roles in the game, but because of the amount of marking, covering and tackling they perform they should have a considerable amount of possession and this demands that their distribution is of a high quality. It is clear that full backs must be very good performers of all the defensive skills, have a thorough understanding of the game and be fit enough to cope with the physical demands of the modern game, particularly on artificial turf.

Traditionally, the FBs would swing according to the position of the ball, with the FB on the same flank as the ball leading and the other covering. As the ball changed sides, so the FBs would follow *(Fig 136)*.

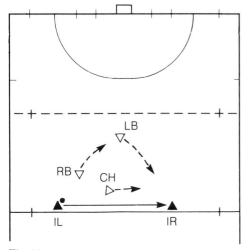

Fig 136

However, there is a third and very important aspect of their role and that is to close down a midfield player if he breaks through (for example an IF as in *Fig 138*). They are helped in this role by their half backs and this part of the combination will be seen in due course.

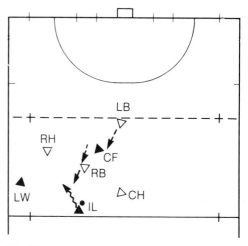

Fig 138

In the modern game, especially on artificial pitches, this traditional method has too many disadvantages and FBs are encouraged to play a more shallow pattern, so that the movement between engaging and covering is far less physically demanding. The FBs have the responsibility between them of marking the CF and covering the defence *(Fig 137)*.

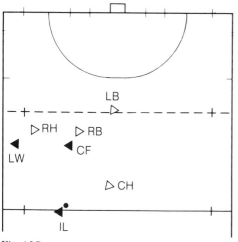

Fig 137

In a situation such as *Fig 138* (the IL beating his midfield opponent) the RB would close down the IL aiming to delay his progress and force him wide if possible. The CH would channel the IL to the RB and threaten any crossfield ball, as well as the gap leading to the CF. The LB would mark the CF even though it would result in both FBs being engaged with little cover. The LB could only afford to stand off the CF if any possibility of a pass was reduced to a minimum. The RH assessing the situation would be best advised to stop any through pass aimed at exploiting the space behind. If the ball is passed in front of the RH to the LW, then it is still well away from the goal and none of the defenders have been beaten.

Fig 139   Even though the Australian defenders were trying to channel the Spanish players towards their LW, the man in possession has been able to counter the move by changing direction in a strong position to exploit the space behind Bestall (No. 4).

Now let us consider a few variations on this situation and suggest the possible responses of the defenders. *Fig 140* shows that the CF is marked by the RB as the IL breaks through. There are a number of possible responses, but the actual movement will depend upon the proximity of particular defenders and their understanding of one another's play.

1. If the CH is close enough he could close in on the IL, allowing the RH and RB to mark and the LB to cover. However, he must not allow the IL to cut back infield.
2. If the IL moves left, the RH and RB could combine to reduce the space available to the IL without opening up easy passes to the LW and CF.
3. If the IL runs quickly at the RB before the CH can cut him off, the RH has to retreat to cover a possible pass to the CF as he moves left, but still infield, of the RH.

As the CF runs laterally, the FBs can pass on the marking role from one to the other, but where it is very likely that a pass will be made as he runs, the marking FB may stay with the CF. In this situation the FBs play like a CB and shallow sweeper.

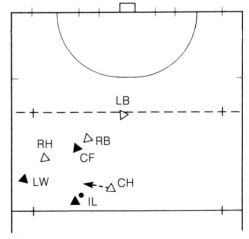

Fig 140

108

The closing down role, performed primarily on the CF and opposing midfield players is helped if the FBs advance up the field as their own team attacks, as not only does this provide support but it also gives them a much greater chance of delaying any counter-attack well upfield, where their own support is most numerous. The danger of engaging so far upfield and playing shallow cover is that a through pass will exploit the space behind the FBs. While this is a possibility, the likelihood can be reduced firstly by the quality of the closing down, delaying and tackling and secondly through a sound understanding between the FB and WH. As the play gets closer to their own circle the marking of the CF will get tighter, but the position of the disengaged FB may vary.

In *Fig 141* the LW has possession and may centre the ball or beat the RH. The CF is marked by the LB and the disengaged FB blocks passes to the danger area in front of goal and covers the RH. If the RH were to be beaten, the RB would close the LW down, leaving the LB, CH

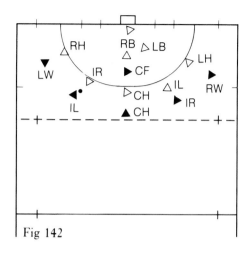

Fig 142

and LH to identify and cover any new danger points. If necessary, the LH would have to leave the RW as the least dangerous forward to move further in the circle to cover a more dangerous position or player. In *Fig 142* the LB has no marking responsibility and, therefore, provides the traditional covering role, but he does not become too isolated from the RB so that the game is as congested as possible (advantageous to the defence) and he is able to respond quickly to changing circumstances. If another attacker appeared in the circle in the IR position, the LB would have to mark him if no one else was available, in which case the LH would drop back a metre or two to provide some cover. This would not be an ideal situation, but the best solution at that particular moment.

Wing Halves

The previous example *(Fig 142)* introduced the wing half into the defending situation and it must be realised that their role is rather different to that of the FB. Wing halves rarely mark their opponents

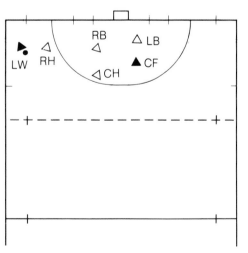

Fig 141

tightly for long as they can only do this when the ball is on their side of the field. When the ball is in the centre of the field and on the opposite flank, the wing half is infield of his winger providing cover to other colleagues rather than marking man to man.

A principle which is sound and true for the majority of cases is: the further the ball is from the wing in question, the more the wing half can cover rather than mark. Having said this, it is imperative that the WH knows where the winger is at all times and is able to counter any moves to use him by either closing the winger down effectively or intercepting the pass directly to the winger or into the space behind the WH. As most passes to the wing come from infield, the WH must have a thorough understanding of where to stand in order to maximise his chances of gaining possession and be able to cover space behind himself and other defenders. A coach can explain all the theory to a player, but the best method of learning positional play is to get out on the field and practise, not only in 1 v 1 situations but also, and more importantly, with

other defenders around.

When the opposition are penetrating the opposite flank, the disengaged WH has some very important decision making to do as he is the only defender who can see the whole situation. His responsibilities will almost certainly extend beyond marking the LW if the LH is beaten or the attacking team manage to get extra men into the attack. In *Fig 143* the RW has beaten the LH who cannot recover. The LB has to go to the RW, but there is no real problem for the RH because the CF is marked by the RB and the CH is a spare defender.

In *Fig 144*, however, the situation is less comfortable. The RW has now eliminated both LH and LB and the defenders are faced with 4 v 3 (+ GK). The danger areas are shaded and these have to be covered by the CH and RH while the RB closes down the RW. Here are some guidelines:

1. There is no need for the RB to rush into a tackle, because there is little chance of the RW scoring with a direct shot. Close the RW down but give nothing

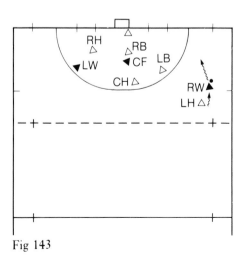

Fig 143

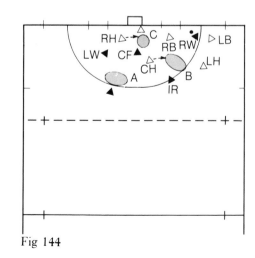

Fig 144

away.

2. The CH can see the danger area B but he does not know what is behind him at the top of the circle (area A). As it is more difficult to score from the edge of the circle than close to goal (area C) the CH may encourage the pass to the IR by leaving the gap open (thereby cutting out any pass to Area A) and only move to intercept as the RW's eyes lower to the ball in order to give the pass.

3. The RH has to move forwards to cover area C making sure that he can cut off or deflect any pass from the RW aimed at the LW.

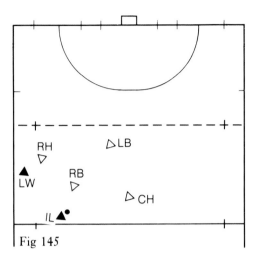

Fig 145

Wing halves must be adept at recognising danger areas and covering them as well as marking. Notice the marking position of the RH in *Fig 143*. He is goal-side and slightly infield of the LW so that he can both see the LW and move to intercept a pass to him, even if the LW moves first!

Wing Halves and Full Back Combination

The previous example gives one illustration of this kind of work, but equally important understanding must take place further upfield especially if the FBs are playing shallow rather than deep cover. The combination play between WH and FB is understandably orientated to coping with penetrative moves and the best way to consider the possible solutions to certain problems is to illustrate examples.

Fig 145 illustrates an FB closing down the IF. As the RB approaches the IL, the RH has to be aware of the fact that going too close to the LW may offer a through pass which could exploit the space behind the defence. The RH, therefore, will position himself so that any early pass

from the IL can only be made directly to the LW who he can then close down quickly, delaying any further move. If the RB is able to stop the IL moving or making an early pass, then the RH will probably be able to tighten his marking of the LW.

In *Fig 146* a through pass has been made to the RW and it is clear that the LH cannot recover quickly enough to stop the RW heading for the circle. The LB moves across to close the space available

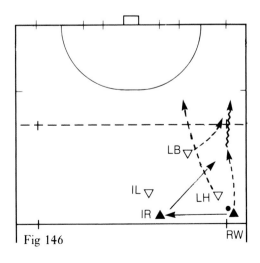

Fig 146

111

to the RW, making sure that the RW cannot cut inside with the ball and is pushed towards the sideline. This will give the other defenders, including the LH, time to cover. Sometimes the FB is able to react early enough to put the ball out or even gain possession, but the priority must be that the RW does not beat the LB.

Fig 147 Here is one for you to think out! The RW beats the LH and cuts infield so that even though the LH is close behind he cannot tackle. What are the alternatives? What factors will influence the responses of the defence?

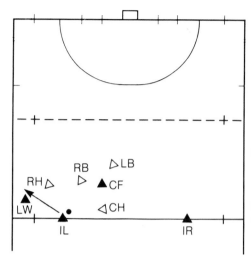
Fig 148

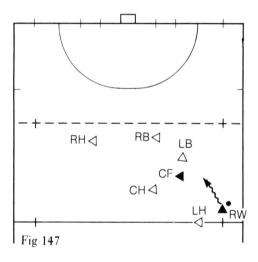
Fig 147

Sometimes it is advantageous for the defence to let the winger have the pass, as it puts the ball in a less dangerous position *(Fig 148)*. It is difficult to state exactly when this is the case, but if the IF could run with the ball beyond the WH before being confronted by another defender or if an even more dangerous situation would arise if the ball was passed infield, then allowing a pass to the wing might well be the least dangerous option. The role of the RH then is to shadow the

winger keeping him as wide as possible, thus allowing covering and marking to occur behind. A really fast or skilful winger can be difficult in these situations, but it may still be the best alternative for the defence.

Team Defence

So far only small groups of players have been studied, but the best defence occurs when all players are participating in harmony and although it may be very rare to get everything perfect (that would make it too easy), good understanding between players goes a long way towards excellent team defence.

What are the priorities when possession is lost?

1. Can the ball be regained immediately?
2. If not, then delay any direct or indirect penetrative pass.
3. Try to keep the ball in the same area of the pitch as it is towards that portion of the field that our players' positions are

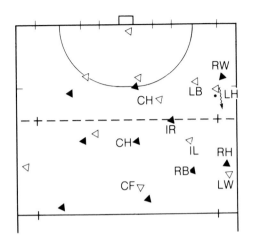

Fig 149

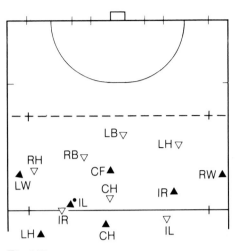

Fig 150

orientated. This will demand the minimum reorientation in order to defend.

The movement of players is best illustrated by an example *(Fig 149)*. The RW has been dispossessed by the LH. If the RW can get back and harass the LH, then he must. The IR has to assess the situation and may decide to close down the LH in order to delay any counter-attack. The CF and CH work to make certain that the ball cannot be switched across field. As the IR moves up on the LH, the RB closes in on the opposing IL and the LB takes the CF. The RH must block any pass to the LW.

This is quite an easy situation but it can be more difficult if the IR or RH are further upfield. What are the options open to the defence now? Think through the factors that would influence the position:

1. Speed of the attackers and therefore the time taken to turn.
2. Movement of the defender with the ball.
3. What priorities has the defender in his mind?
4. Where are the best passes for the defender?
5. Can we leave open the least advantageous pass? Which one is it?
6. Is it best to delay their attack by closing the LH down or standing off? When would you do the latter? (*Clue* When you open up more passes beyond you by going towards him.)

Study *Fig 150;* white IR has been dispossessed by black IL. What are the responses of the white team?

Two simple concepts that have been successfully used in the coaching of defence to England and Great Britain players in recent years have been:

'Defend from the front.'

'Defending begins just before the opposition gains possession.'

113

Fig 151 Tom Van t'Heck prepares to change direction quickly.
Note the concentration of both players on the ball, and
the poise, balance and technique of Van t'Heck as he
makes the reverse stick play. (Netherlands v New
Zealand, Los Angeles 1984)

114

7 Tactics at Set Pieces and Restarts

There are over 100 set pieces and restarts in a hockey match!

Inextricably bound up with the offensive and defensive tactics in open play are the tactical manoeuvres and responses at restarts and set pieces. Hockey has a large number of stoppages, however short, and during that time the defending team can reorganise. The response of the attacking team must be to have a number of rehearsed manoeuvres that can be utilised according to the situation. In this way the team in possession can hopefully maintain the pressure on the defenders in spite of the latter's organisation. The defensive team, however, are determined to nullify any attacking ploy either immediately or before a significant advantage can be gained. It can be seen, therefore, that the battle is as much intellectual – anticipating, recognising and countering the opposition's moves – as it is technical and physical. A team that has only one solution to a problem is quite easily countered and so any set piece must have a number of variations. The challenge is recognising and using the one that is the key to solving the problem in that particular situation.

I have taken five situations – penalty corners; corners; free hits in the defensive zone; restarts from the sideline; free hits in the attacking zone – and attempt to give some ideas for both the attack and the defence. If I err towards the former, it is merely that I like to see the defence made to work hard! There are instances when I have deliberately not given the answers to some problems, as I feel it important that you should use the concepts discussed and your own experience to practise the areas of decision making that are required of both coaches and players alike. Throughout this chapter it is assumed that the previous chapters have been studied, as it is impossible to put down all the individual moves, skills, and so on.

When a coach wishes to develop these or other moves invented by coach and players, then please follow the guidelines to progressive practices given in Chapter 1. It is wasteful of time and players to involve everyone right from the beginning.

PENALTY CORNERS

Defending Penalty Corners

As only four players and the goalkeeper are allowed back, the distribution of personnel is critical. If, in addition to pressurising the striker, the defence wishes to cover the danger areas shown in *Fig 152*, then some important decisions have to be taken. It is not difficult to see that if the GK stands in the traditional position, it is very difficult to distribute four men to cover the danger areas A to E. The options open to the defence include the following:

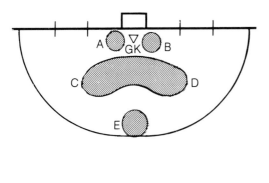

Fig 152

1. The GK does not play traditionally. He may come out considerably further to narrow the angle of the shot, perhaps even closing down the striker himself *(Fig 153)*. If he performs the latter skill then he must have a man either side of him in support, otherwise he can be bypassed too easily. If the GK comes out 7 to 8 metres rather than 4 to 5 metres, he may pressurise the striker to hit wide but the opportunity for him to react to a good shot is less, so the corners of the goal are still vulnerable.

Top-class GKs on artificial turf are

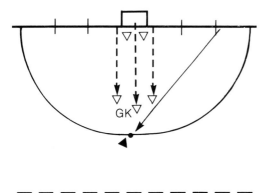

Fig 153

coming out and lying down at the corner so that only one player on the line is required (on the GK's head side), as the commonly accepted interpretation of the rule governing the first hit at goal is that it must be below the eighteen inch back-boards and the vast majority of strikes can be saved. This is an advanced technique and must only be attempted with the correct equipment and coaching. I dislike seeing schoolboys use this method and would advise them to learn the fundamentals of goalkeeping before considering these advanced ploys.

2. The GK stands up as normal and the defenders leave the striker to strike unhindered *(Fig 154)*. This gives the defence the advantage of covering the

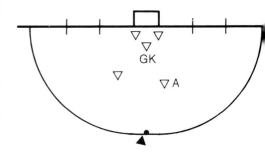

Fig 154

danger points closest to the goal, but the disadvantage of a free shot. Player A in this formation would be the closest to the striker and ready to move forward if the striker were to try and bring the ball in before making a shot.

3. As in 2, but leave only one man on the line and have a man harassing the striker *(Fig 155)*. The position of player A could vary according to the ability of the

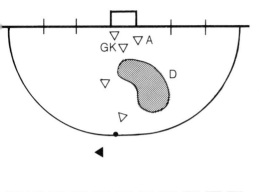

Fig 155

GK to cover that post and the ability of the man on the line to cover perhaps a yard of the goal near the other post. If the post needs covering, player A needs to be on the correct line but far enough out to cover the danger area D. A defensive advantage of reducing the number of players on or near the goal line is that an offside line is automatically introduced. I suppose this offside line could be pushed some distance out from goal, but I fear that a mad rush forward by the defence would only work once!

To help coaches and players decide on their method, they need to consider the following factors:

1. With only five defenders it is important to concentrate attention on the most dangerous areas of the circle as indicated in *Fig 152*. This is not to say that the other parts of the circle cannot be used effectively, merely that shots from there are a little less dangerous.
2. A ball passed from left to right at the top of the circle takes longer to control and strike than after a pass from right to left, when an immediate shot is possible. Therefore, if a space is to be left open,

perhaps the area on the left of the defence is preferable (see area D in *Fig 152*).
3. Runners out should make every effort *not* to cross the GK's line of sight (*Fig 156*).
4. The runner out should be ready to slow up if it is evident that he cannot charge down the shot or the opposition are going to move the ball, otherwise he will be unable to help his defence in the second or third phases of the penalty corner. He should run so that he is to the left of the ball as it is stopped. This presents his forehand stick to the ball and partially closes off passes to the attacking team's right.

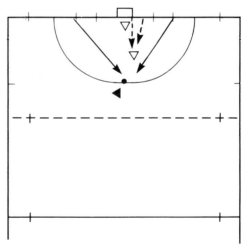

Fig 156

5. On artificial surfaces the ball travels much faster, giving GKs less time in which to react.
6. Each defensive role at penalty corners is a special one and players must be chosen according to the demands of that role. Consider the roles carefully and practise them.

117

Fig 157 Jon Potter clears the ball after a penalty corner. (Great Britain v Pakistan, Perth 1985)

Attacking Moves at Penalty Corners

There are innumerable variations, but it is sensible to consider the following factors before options are chosen:

1. The ball must be stopped dead before the first shot.
2. There may be an offside trap.
3. It is more difficult to score from a wide position in the circle.
4. The defenders cannot cover all the danger points.
5. A hard accurate strike is still a fearful weapon.
6. The greater the number of passes, the greater the likelihood of error.

7. How is the ball going to be stopped? Does this affect the options possible?

The following diagrams illustrate some ideas for penalty corners, but it may be as important to consider an effective defence against each one.

Hit out from RW and stopped on reverse stick (Fig 158). The options are:

1. Direct shot.
2. and 3. Striker (B) dribbles left or right of runner out if he comes too fast when the stick stopper has made a good stop.
4. Stick stopper (A) pulls ball to right after he has stopped it. He can shoot or, if the runner follows him, slip the ball back

for the striker.

5. Striker (B) deliberately hits the ball outside the right post where the injecter has moved to. The man can deflect the ball at goal.

Dummy hits and flicks by the striker can be incorporated.

nearest defender and by the deception put on the pass.

6. A pass to the RW who has come onside and in towards the goal. This pass can be deflected at goal, controlled before a shot or, if there are two men on the goal line, played across the face of the goal to the middle where the LW can be waiting.

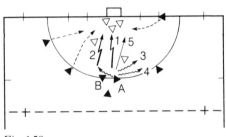

Fig 158

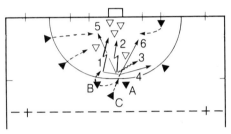

Fig 159

Hit out from RW and stopped on the reverse stick but this time the striker (B) moves left and the support player (C) steps in (Fig 159). The advantages of this move are that the support player can concentrate upon the position of the defenders rather than the ball, and the movement left of the striker will make the GK reorientate if the ball is passed left.

The options include:

1. The ball is slipped left for the striker to shoot or dribble and then shoot.
2. The support player may shoot.
3. The support player dribbles to the right and then shoots.
4. The ball is passed right to the player in the IR position, who can shoot, dribble in and slip the ball left to the striker or support player about ten metres from the goal.
5. The ball is played to the LW. This move is made possible by the CF staying out and attracting the attention of the

These moves could be modified for an upright stick stop when the hit out is from the LW. Encourage players to be inventive but assess the potential of the moves carefully. The best routines have a number of alternatives based upon a single ploy.

When a team is practising penalty corners it is important to remember that the moves, both attacking and defending, need to be done initially without too much competition and separately; it is not sensible to practise both attack and defence simultaneously. A competition of barrages of five corners, properly umpired, is good for concentrating the players' minds, but it must be used sparingly.

CORNERS

The attacking side will look to pressurise the defence by playing the ball into one of

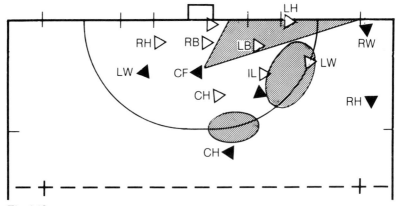

Fig 160

the three shaded areas unless there is an obvious pass to an unmarked attacker in the circle *(Fig 160)*. The area nearest the goal line can, if penetrated, produce a deflected shot at goal or a difficult situation for a defender trying to control the ball leading to a goal scoring opportunity or a penalty corner. The two shaded areas on the edge of the circle can be used by attacking players as they can control the ball on the forehand stick and pressurise a defender on his reverse stick side or play the ball towards goal for the CF. The IR can move towards the goal on the goal-

side of his opponent and then step out towards the edge of the circle as the ball is played to him. The CH can use a similar move *(Fig 161)* or, if the IR stays in the circle, move towards the RW.

Defensively the line-up can be as shown in *Fig 160*, where the LW is threatening the passes to the IR and CH while the LH and LB are positioned so that they are nearer the ball than other attackers but far enough away to control the ball. Getting too close is rather fool-hardy as a player rarely stops anything. The attack may play the ball short to the RH, but that immediately changes the situation and the LW would close him down rapidly.

One possible alternative is for the LH and LB to take up slightly different positions, with both players the same distance from the ball as shown in *Fig 160*, but now the LB covers the pass close to the baseline while the LH positions himself two or three metres infield from the baseline. The advantages of this formation are that the LH is able to force the hitter to play the ball further away from goal, because the large gap on the LH's reverse stick is covered by the LB's forehand stick and the LB's reverse stick

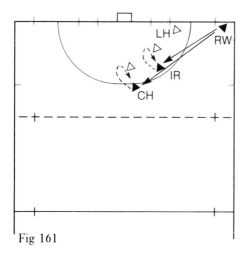

Fig 161

s covered by the GK.

Similar defensive patterns can be established for corners from the LW, and the attacking moves could include the five shown in *Fig 162* and briefly described below.

1. LW passes to a support player who dribbles as if to go round the forehand stick of the defender but who plays the ball to the LW who has looped behind his colleague.
2. The IL, or player who best finds space when marked tightly, manipulates the opponent and receives a hard pass onto his open stick. The skill is to let the ball come right across the body in order to exploit the reverse stick side.
3. The IL deliberately pulls the defender towards the edge of the circle and a similar pass to that in 2 above is played to the CF as he moves towards the ball.
4. As in 3 above, but the IL keeps the man inside the circle and the ball goes to the CH.
5. If the RH is weak, or the gap is there, then a pass to the CF is very dangerous for the defence.

FREE HITS

General

If it is advantageous to take free hits quickly then do so wherever they are on the field. The key to successful quick free hits is in providing the opportunity for the ball to penetrate a line of the opposing defence, whether it be twenty metres or seventy metres from their goal. The concepts are very simple even though they require expert skills and timing to succeed at the highest level:

1. Providing support ahead of the ball *(Fig 163)*.

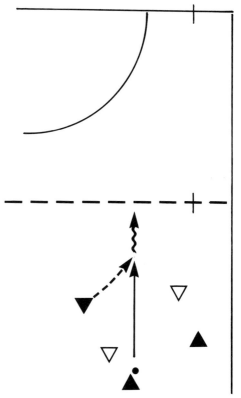

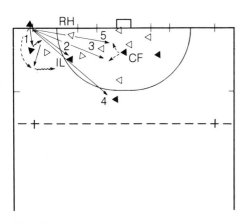

Fig 162

Fig 163

2. Providing space ahead of the ball (*Fig 164*). (The attacker takes his close marker away from the area.)

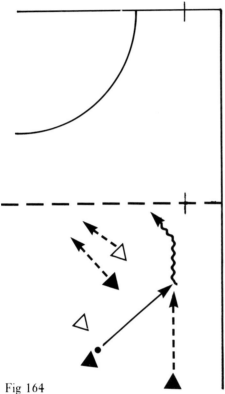

Fig 164

These situations only exist for a short time, so players must be encouraged to look for them and then coached to time the movements perfectly.

The second general point might seem to contradict the previous one, but on consideration it does not; sometimes free hits have only been gained after a great deal of hard work so do not throw away possession by a rash decision.

Thirdly, it is important to recognise whether the opposition are marking man to man or zonally. In the former situation a defender may be deliberately enticed away from an area that is to be utilised by the same attacker or a colleague, and the crucial skills are the timings of the movement of the receiver and the pass so that sufficient space has been created to make the next move. When zonal marking is encountered the defenders are less concerned with the movement of the players and more orientated to cover the spaces into which the ball is likely to travel with the intention of intercepting it. The crucial skills in this situation are the ability to pass accurately and with deception to beat the potential interceptors and the intelligent movement of the receivers.

Finally, all players must understand these general points concerning free hits and make use of the knowledge; even I have noticed that marking gets tighter at free hits inside the opposition's final 35 metres and any moves to beat them must be extremely well timed!

In the Defensive Zone

The majority of free hits in defence are taken level with the top of the circle and the objective is to get the ball going forward and directly or indirectly into the midfield area.

The options include:

1. A short free hit to another defender who can move forward. The crucial point is that he must be able to move forwards with the ball as this is more likely to cause the opposition difficulties in intercepting the passes. The forward movement must be such that he can make a pass whenever it is required.
2. A free hit to the RW (*Fig 165*). Angled passes to the RW can be made after he has moved backwards along the sideline and/or infield towards the passer

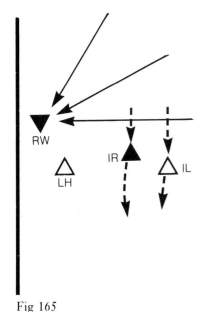

Fig 165

of the ball. The IR can help this pass by moving upfield with his marker.

Coaching points

* Control the ball and turn to face opponent.
* Time the backward move to create space.
* Use the infield movement to expose the reverse stick side of the LH.
* Look for passes to IR, CH and CF.

A straight pass can be made to the RW's reverse stick from the RH but this will usually follow a previous pass to the RH. For this pass to be successful, the RW would have to pull his marker infield and then turn back towards the sideline.

If the IR moves out to receive a pass from the RB position and he is tightly marked, a pass may be available to the RW running infield and slightly forwards. The timing has to be excellent as this pass will have to be hit hard *(Fig 166)*.

3. A free hit to the IR. In *Fig 167* the RH picks out the forehand stick of the IR

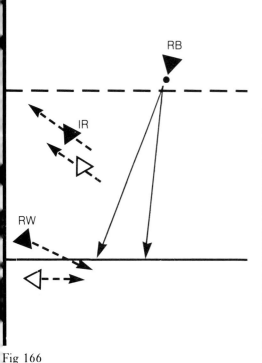

Fig 166

RH

IR

Fig 167

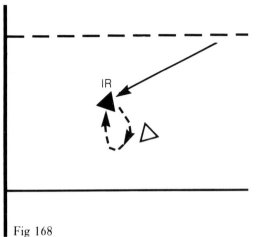

Fig 168

as he moves back and slightly towards the RH. The objective is to retain possession and keep the ball going forwards. If the IR is not closely marked the pass could be given to his reverse stick, but the IR must show the target.

Passes from the central area of the defence can be taken on either the forehand stick as the IR moves slightly backwards and outside of his marker (*Fig 168*) or the reverse stick as he turns

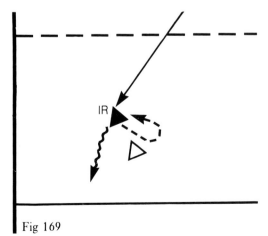

Fig 169

quickly in an anticlockwise direction *(Fig 169)*.

If the pass is coming from the CH position, then it is most effective if both the CH and the IR are moving forward as this causes the defenders to run backwards and it is then easier to use deception successfully *(Fig 170)*. Notice the movement of the players and consider the speed, position and timing of the pass.

The basic concepts hold good for the left side of the field and moves can be developed quite easily for the IL and LW

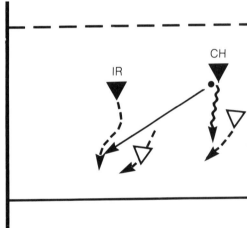

Fig 170

provided that players and coaches remember that passes to the left are mostly on the forehand stick side of defenders and therefore require greater care, precision and timing to be effective. On either side of the field interchange of positions can open up spaces for the pass but it is vital that these are practised so that all the players involved can recognise the cues.

n the Attacking Zone

During a season coaches and players see o many free hits in the attacking zone wasted unnecessarily that one begins to despair, but it is only fair to assess the problems faced by the attackers before any basic ideas are suggested. The following are some of the problems:

1. Any opening will not remain open for long.
2. The ball is moving or has to be placed on the right spot.
3. Colleagues are over-anxious and move too early or call poorly.
4. The passer, perhaps frustrated by the opposition, tries a foolish pass.
5. There are more defenders than attackers.
6. The area is congested, putting great emphasis upon the quality of the pass.
7. The passer concentrates on the ball rather than looking for a pass.
8. Players may not use any relevant previous experience, for example a particular defender does not mark tightly or the opposition have stopped every hard cross ball into the circle.

No doubt there are plenty of others too, but the principal reasons for the breakdown are that all too often the attacking players are under intense pressure and they have no basic structure of what they can do in these situations on which to fall back in their moment of need. That is why so many teams set up so many free hits so slowly – to perform a known pattern!

If a number of small-scale patterns between two or three players can be established, then they will have a repertoire with which to tackle the problem.

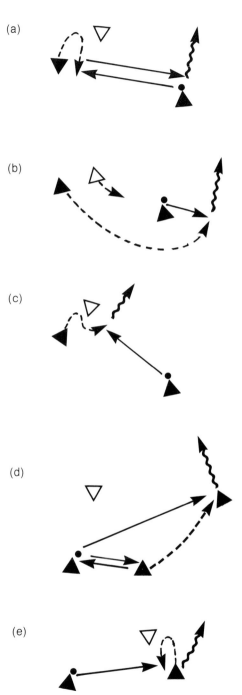

(a)

(b)

(c)

(d)

(e)

Fig 171

This is not to negate the place in attacking free hits of either the risk-taking move between two players or the slower set piece involving many players of both teams, but rarely do either of these two produce goals. There must be a large half-way house between these two extremes in which a simple but rehearsed pattern could transform a frustrated attack into a goal scoring opportunity. *Fig 171* may provide a few ideas in addition to those put forward in the general points on free hits. Many of these can be used to restart the game quickly in order to set up a 2 v 1.

Coaching questions:
1. What are the cues to set up the move?
2. Who initiates it?
3. Timing of the pass?
4. Position of the pass?

There are, however, a considerable number of times around the circle when a free hit cannot be taken quickly. This does not in any way exclude the use of any of the ideas so far described, but it would be unrealistic not to illustrate one or two common manoeuvres even if they only serve to help consider the defensive side of the coin.

Fig 172 shows the CH striking a free hit hard to the forehand stick of the IR who has previously moved his marker into the circle and then retreated smartly as the hit is made. The IR initiates the move. The RW stays wide to hold the LH out. The aim of the IR is to exploit the reverse side of the marker or project the ball into the shaded area towards which the CF will be moving.

Consider the defence of this situation. What instructions could be given to the marker of the IR? Could the CH threaten the pass? If he does, how do the attacker respond? If there was an extra defender back, where should he stand?

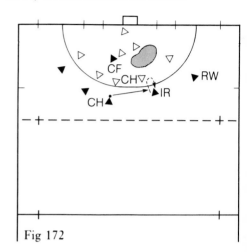

Fig 172

Another example is given in *Figs 173 & 174* but this time the pass is from right to left. In the first move (*Fig 173*) the IL moves into the circle and then retreats to receive a pass on his forehand stick and looks to drive into the circle. The second move (*Fig 174*) is based on the previous one but in this case the IL stays in the circle and the LW cuts across for the ball onto his forehand stick. Signals, timings

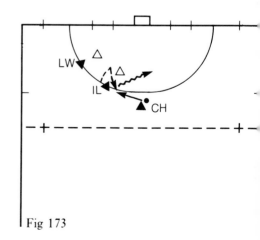

Fig 173

126

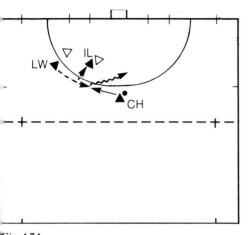

Fig 174

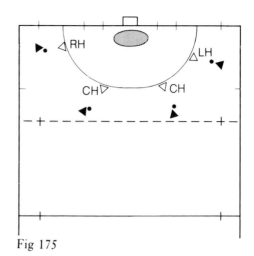

Fig 175

ues and targets have to be carefully worked out to guarantee success. Consider the defence again and think through the possible responses to these moves.

Finally, turning to the defending side, there is no substitute for getting the team lined up as if to defend a free hit and demand that they comment upon their positions; modify them if necessary and practise coping with a variety of free hits. All teams would ideally like to be able to put an attacking free hit into the circle to an unmarked player who controls the ball and scores a goal. Sadly for the attackers, the defenders object to this ploy and work to stop the ball reaching the attackers or particularly dangerous areas. *Fig 175* illustrates one particularly dangerous zone in the circle which is about four metres out from goal. If a free hit can penetrate to this area the GK is vulnerable to any slight deflection by an attacker. To help protect this area either one of the WHs or the CH lines up directly between the ball and the zone, covering as much of the area with the body and forehand stick as is possible. This position, particularly for WHs,

should be called by the GK. Once this man is in position, the locations of the other defenders can be determined quickly in accordance with the marking and covering requirements.

RESTARTS FROM SIDELINE

The principal objective must be to retain possession and the experimental rule allowing members of the side in possession to be as close to the injector as they please certainly makes this an easily attainable objective, initially anyway. However, there are a few simple objectives that influence this restart. Firstly, it is unwise in the defensive third of the pitch to take unnecessary risks from this restart as an interception could lead to a rapid and potentially dangerous counterattack as the player taking the hit-in is not in a very good defensive position in relation to his goal. For this reason many restarts in this area are put close to the touch line and even though a man in close support widens the angle, safety is still a

127

major concern. In fact, players should question the wisdom of playing a pass from any position along the sideline that, if intercepted, would result in the opposition having the ball in a situation that exposes their own defence (for example *Fig 176*).

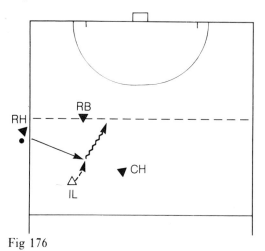

Fig 176

Secondly, it is rare to be able to play a really incisive pass from this kind of restart, whether it be a short or long pass, and the priority in the midfield and attacking zones should be to keep possession, maintain the pressure on the defensive team and use the possession to set up subsequent penetrative moves (*see* the sections on passing, attacking tactics and free hits).

While the ruling is that the team in possession can go as close to the injector as they wish, it is best to consider the hit-in as a free hit and use the same considerations and ploys illustrated in that section. However, if the five metre ruling returns, coaches must consider rehearsed ploys to overcome the closeness of the opponents' marking.

The first ploy is to take players away

from the area to establish whether the opposition are going to mark man to man or zonally or a mixture of both. If the opposition mark man to man, create space by moving away from the ball and then returning to receive a pass or leaving the space for a colleague to use. If, however, zonal marking is employed then the players should seek to exploit the space behind and on the reverse stick side of the opponents surrounding the hit-in. This requires intelligent movement and high quality passing. Consider how to mark zonally without creating these weaknesses.

Figs 177, 179 and *181* illustrate some other basic ploys for hit-ins that are relevant whether or not the experimental rule becomes law.

In *Fig 177* the RW comes infield to draw the LH from the line and create space to receive a pass on either the forehand or reverse stick. The RW can play the ball back to the RH, attack the reverse stick of the LH or even draw the LH further infield to allow a pass to be made into the space along the sideline.

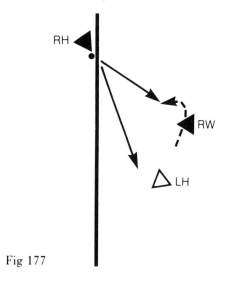

Fig 177

Fig 178 Blöcher (West Germany) pounces on a loose ball at a
defensive penalty corner and sweeps it away before the
Pakistan forward can make contact.

In *Fig 179* the IR makes space to receive
the pass after which the options include.

1. Pass back to RH.
2. Beat the opponent.
3. Pass infield to CH or another colleague.

Fig 181 illustrates a more difficult move
for the LW and LH. The LW stands
infield of the RH, which is unusual to
start with. The response of the RH may
be to try and position himself behind the
LW. The LW now moves infield and
then away from the ball turning anticlockwise as he moves away. If the RH
has moved with him there will be a gap

Fig 179

129

Fig 180   An interesting one for the umpires. There is no doubt
that, whatever the decision, one of the players
(Charlesworth and Fried) was disappointed. (Australia
v Germany, 1982)

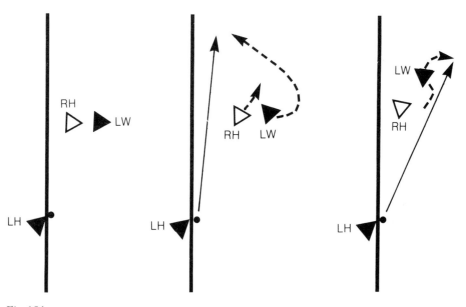

Fig 181

along the line and the LH sends the ball through it for the LW to run on to. However, if the RH anticipates the move and steps to his right to close the gap then the LH keeps the ball. If as the LW turns to face the side the ball has not arrived, he will know that the gap has been closed and that the LH will now play the alternative pass infield of the RH and onto the LW's reverse stick.

All these ploys seek primarily to retain possession, although the last is quite incisive (but difficult!), and coaches and players must study the defensive aspect of these moves. How can we make it as difficult as possible for the opposition? How are they likely to respond to our defensive tactics?

CONCLUSION

Restarts and set pieces are numerous in a game of hockey and it is good coaching to spend time planning and practising both the attack and the defence of them. The simplest moves are the best, but even these take a great deal of thought and preparation if they are to work in the very pressured environment of a game. When practising any of the set pieces discussed in this chapter, make certain that the progressions are carefully planned so that the players are learning at the right speed or are succeeding at ever-increasing levels of stress.

Fig 182   The West German goalkeeper makes himself as large a
barrier as possible to the likely pass of the Australian
forward.

8 Coaching for Goalkeepers

Almost a game within a game.

Until recently little attention has been paid to the coaching of goalkeepers. The harassed schoolmaster would generally place his least skilful, least mobile player in goal and leave him to teach himself, concentrating on other players in positions he knew most about. The situation is now changing rapidly with the realisation that the goalkeeper is perhaps the *most* important player in the team, for, if he has a 'shut-out' the team cannot lose! There are very special, almost unique, skills involved in hockey goalkeeping and this chapter is aimed at being a first step towards developing the skills required.

GOALKEEPING QUALITIES

The individual skills involved in hockey goalkeeping call for a cross between Alan Knott and Ray Clemence – cat-like agility with a bit of beef!

The coach should aim to develop and improve the following qualities in the goalkeeper and design a programme containing the correct balance of these qualities: skill; agility; mobility; speed; stamina; strength; concentration; and confidence. The exercises in the training programme should incorporate training for as many of these qualities as possible. The mindful coach will attempt to devise new exercises to stimulate and improve his goalkeeper.

Logically, if the ball does not enter the net then the goalkeeper is performing his function. Good technique, however, will obviously decrease his percentage of error and raise his *skill level*.

Figs 183 and *184* show the right way and the wrong way of saving a ball with the pads. The crucial point is *balance* – important in all ball games. In *Fig 183* the goalkeeper has fallen backwards and his weight is badly positioned. In *Fig 184* he has begun from a well-balanced position *(see Fig 186)* and has driven from this starting point to save the ball in the

Fig 183

Fig 184

Fig 185

stretch position. Note these coaching points:

1. The position of the head is forward, aiding balance.
2. After the save has been made, the goalkeeper is on his feet ready for the next shot.

The correct balance position can again be seen in *Fig 185* where the goalkeeper has saved the ball with his left leg at a fair height from the ground. He has driven off from his starting point *(Fig 186)* and will land, ready to deal with the next shot. It is clear from these pictures of the need for *agility* and *mobility* training described later in the chapter.

All goalkeeping skills stem from the classic position of readiness *(Fig 186)*. From this position the ball can be stopped by bringing the pads together and cushioning the impact of the ball by bending the knees slightly. The ball can then be propelled away using either foot or stick (one-handed or two). Remember that the

Fig 186

Fig 187

Fig 188

Fig 189

Fig 190

best method of clearing the ball with the stick is by using a flick or push. It is quicker and easier than a hit.

The goalkeeper should also be encouraged to develop the 'save-clear' technique of propelling the ball away as it arrives. By propelling his weight through the ball as already seen in *Figs 183* and *184*, and shown clearly in *Fig 187*, the ball will be away from the danger area, preventing any follow-up opportunity. Note:

1. Balance is essential.
2. The head should be well forward and the eyes following the ball.

Figs 188 to 190 show the correct method of saving with the hand and stick on either side of the body. Again *balance* and *head position* are the keys to success, and an ability to get back to the position of readiness as quickly as possible. Note that when saving on the right-hand side, the stick remains in the right hand and the left hand comes across *(Fig 189)*. This is similar to the way a soccer goalkeeper saves the ball. *Fig 190* shows a similar technique with the ball higher than the shoulder: the *left* hand is making the save. The reason for not transferring the stick into the left hand is simply that the goalkeeper probably will not have time. The latter skill should be practised, however.

Training of the techniques so far outlined will develop the qualities mentioned earlier and improve the goalkeeper. Training practices are referred to later.

Figs 191 to 194 show various methods of taking the ball in a 1 v 1 situation. *Fig 191* shows the slide tackle. *Fig 192* shows the reverse stick tackle and *Fig 193* the open side tackle. *Fig 194* shows the goalkeeper spreading himself having anticipated a shot. He has placed as much

135

Fig 191

Fig 192

Fig 193

Fig 194

of his body as possible between the goal and the ball.

Coaching points:
1. Head position in all *Figs* should be noted.
2. The goalkeeper is wearing a mask – this is essential.
3. He is fearless – an essential condition in goalkeeping brought about by confidence and concentration on the position of the ball.

Individual Training

Some qualities required by goalkeepers can be aided by individual training.

AGILITY AND MOBILITY

Agility and mobility can be improved by *yoga-style* stretching exercises, concentrating on the back, hips and legs. As a rule, spend time stretching daily: stretch very slowly, going down to the point of pain, hold for five seconds and then press a little further. Repeat each exercise three times.

SPEED

Speed can be improved by springing, particularly short distances. The goalkeeper moves a lot sideways and the *sideways shuttle* should be practised. Set up four posts – two at goal width with one at either end – two metres from each 'goal-post'. The goalkeeper shuttles sideways as though moving across his goal, goes round the end post and back in a figure-of-eight motion *(Fig 195)*. Each shuttle should be completed three times, as quickly as possible, before a rest of thirty seconds. The exercise should be

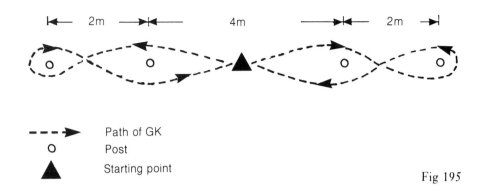

- - - →   Path of GK
  O   Post
  ▲   Starting point

Fig 195

repeated six times.

Fig 196 shows the '*points of a compass*' *shuttle*. This is designed to simulate the goalkeeper coming off his line to save a penalty corner. He begins at the centre post and moves forward going round the 'northern' post, keeping his back to it. He aims to set himself briefly, as though to save a shot, as he passes the 'northern' post. Then he returns to the centre, before continuing round the 'eastern', 'southern' and 'western' points. When he arrives at the centre post again he repeats the exercise – anticlockwise – and completes one shuttle. Again, repeat the exer-

cise six times with a rest of thirty seconds between each run. *Note*: The goalkeeper should always keep his back to the centre post – having passed each point, he moves *backwards* to the centre.

STAMINA

Stamina is not as important as for field players, but the goalkeeper needs a certain amount for training effectively. It can be built up by training; but running, say three miles once or twice a week, will aid general fitness.

STRENGTH

Leg strength is important and can be improved by weight training. Speed weight training, which will also improve reaction time and speed, is the correct method. The goalkeeper should have a circuit devised, concentrating on the stomach and legs, but not ignoring the other main muscle groups. This is made up of exercises incorporating the maximum weight he can lift seven times. He then performs his circuit, made up of each exercise completed five times, as quickly as possible. He does three circuits.

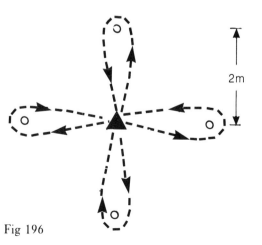

Fig 196

2m

137

PRACTICES

The enthusiastic coach will be forever developing his own practices, but here are a few incorporating the *skills* outlined earlier:

1. After warming-up the goalkeeper stands in a goal and the feeder, kneeling five to seven metres away, throws tennis or hockey balls low to either side alternately. The goalkeeper saves with alternate feet, aiming to 'save-clear' (*see Fig 187*).

2. As in 1, but the ball is thrown at knee height (*see Fig 185*).

3. As in 1 and 2, but the feeder throws where he pleases, not dummying and allowing the goalkeeper to regain his central position prior to throwing the next ball.

4. As in 1 and 2, but the feeder throws at about waist height. The goalkeeper saves as in *Figs 188* and *189*.

5. As in 1 and 2, but higher still so that the goalkeeper saves as in *Fig 186*.

6. As in 3, but the goalkeeper uses only his hand or stick.

7. As in 3, but the feeder may throw to either foot or hand/stick.

8. The feeder now hits the ball from about ten metres to one side constantly so that the goalkeeper can practise his techniques, particularly the save-clear technique as in *Fig 187*.

9. Two players are now used together with the feeder as in *Fig 197*. The feeder (F) hits the ball at the goalkeeper who rebounds to the players, P1 and P2. They play the ball back at the goalkeeper. The aim is to keep the ball in play as long as possible. As the players and goalkeeper become more skilled, the speed can be increased and a competitive element in-troduced, i.e. scoring as many goals as possible.

10. A player receives the ball outside the circle from a feeder, positioned on one side of the 22 metre area. He beats a semi-passive opponent at the top of or just inside the circle and attempts to take on the goalkeeper who tries to tackle him as in *Figs 191 to 194. Note:* The goalkeeper must anticipate the action and attempt to 'take' the player having moved off his line.

11. As in 10, but this time the semi-passive player is outside the circle and the player shoots having crossed the line. The goalkeeper remains near his line, having moved off to narrow the angle, and attempts to save the shot.

12. As in 11, but two follow-up players attempt to pick up the rebound and score. Unlike in 9, the goalkeeper is attempting to remove the ball from danger as quickly as possible.

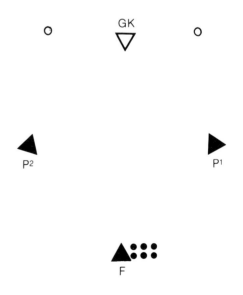

Fig 197

Fig 198 James Duthie flicks at goal. Notice his body position, the reaction of the goalkeeper, the defender's attempted tackle and the support of Sean Kerly. (Great Britain v West Germany, Olympic semi-final, Los Angeles 1984)

The practices outlined here have been built up progressively. In order to help develop goalkeeping qualities, all training should be progressive. This will build confidence as the goalkeeper sees himself improving.

The modern technique of lying down at penalty corners has deliberately been excluded; I make no apology for this omission as I am unhappy that young players should attempt the technique before they have learnt the fundamentals of goalkeeping. No young man should be expected to perform this technique unless he is provided with the *best* coaching and the *best* equipment. I suggest that coaches experience it themselves before they try and convince others to do it! When a player is adult and can rationally assess the requirements and the problems, then that is a different situation.

Fig 199   Great Britain's Jimmy Duthie beats two defenders on his
way into the Indian circle. Note the hand positions and
the foot placement.

9 Assessing Teams and Players

A team is as strong as its weakest player.

There are two important and distinctly different roles within this sphere of work. The first is the continuous assessment of the players within and aspiring to the squad, while the second is the assessment of the teams that are to be the opponents in a match or tournament.

SQUAD PLAYERS

It is impossible for a coach to stand back and be completely dispassionate concerning the abilities of all the players, but it is important to be as objective as possible. The function of the exercise is to assess the particular strengths and weaknesses in a player's game so that during the next period of coaching the weaknesses can be improved and the strengths utilised in team play. Many of the abilities a coach wishes to assess can be viewed in carefully planned practices, small-sided games or matches, but to get as complete a picture as possible at least two of these should be used. In addition to observation, data can be collected concerning any of the skills, physical tests may be given and the scores/times recorded, questionnaires can cast light on the psychological aspects and discussion may add many small but important pieces of information – all of which when put together provide a comprehensive study of the player. In reality, however, few coaches have the resources to do all of

these things and I put forward the following simple check list which, if done properly, may still take a considerable time for each player. It is sometimes difficult to concentrate upon assessing an individual in a match as one is attracted to watch the ball, but it is a skill a coach must master if he is to give valid assessments of players.

THE OPPOSITION

Ideally it is best to watch the opposition several times before your team meets them, but rarely is this possible. Even so the following areas may give you an indication of what to analyse.

Team Assessment

TEAM FORMATION

1. What system are they playing?
2. What marking do they employ?

STYLE OF PLAY

1. Do they generally prefer to initiate attacks or do they wait for the counter-attack opportunities?
2. Do they tend to attack on one flank or in one particular way?
3. Do they defend a lead or carry on as before?
4. How do they defend?

Areas of Study	Particular Aspects	Strengths?	Weaknesses?
On the ball skills	Control — open — reverse Passing — hit — push — aerial — reverse Running with ball Vision with ball Beating a man — forehand — reverse		
Off the ball skills	Marking — man to man — zonal Covering Supporting attack Closing down Tackling — forehand — reverse		
Reading the game	Does he anticipate events?		
Physical abilities	Stamina Speed Strength Mobility		
Temperament	Concentration Aggression Attitude		

Fig 200

PARTICULAR PLAYERS

1. Where are their key attacking players?
2. Who are their important ball winners?

PLAYING RHYTHM/SPEED

1. Do they concentrate upon fast attacks or slow patient build-up?
2. Do they attack leaving their defenders deep or does the whole team step up the field?

SET PIECES

1. Do they have particular moves at free hits, short corners, and so on?
2. Can these moves be anticipated?

TACTICS

1. Are there any particular tactics generally used, for example aerial passes, long passes to a particular player, short inter-passing between certain players?

Individual Assessment

This analysis must be done for both on and off the ball skills *(Fig 200)*.

TECHNICAL ABILITY

1. How does he control the ball?
2. What are his favourite passes?
3. How does he beat a player?
4. What stick and body feints does he use?
5. How does he close down and tackle?
6. Are there weaknesses or predictable moves in these areas that can be used to our advantage?

FITNESS

1. Speed and endurance?
2. How quickly can he turn?

TEMPERAMENT

How does he react to various forms of pressure, for example tight marking, closing down, lack of possession, the team performing poorly?

Players should be encouraged to watch and assess their opposing players and the other opposition players in their positions, as both these sets of comments can provide important information. At international level we pool this knowledge at team meetings and find it highly informative, about both the opposition *and* our own players! It may sound trite, but be careful not to draw too many conclusions concerning team play from watching the future opponents play against a team with a very different style to your own; be selective in your analysis.

Fig 201 Kallimullah (Pakistan), one of the outstanding left wingers of the late 1970s, cuts in towards the Netherlands' circle using the forehand stick, willed on by a large number of his countrymen.

143

Fig 202 While Billy McLean has a rest, the author prays that David
Owen cuts out the centre! (Great Britain v India, Karachi 1980)

TACTICAL PLANNING

Finally, this information is used to formulate team tactics and individual roles for
the forthcoming game. The actual tactics
will depend upon the information accum-
ulated and the views and objectives of the
team management, but the thought pro-
cesses ought to be similar for all matches.
Here are some of the questions I go
through when developing a tactical plan
for both individuals and the team.

When They Have the Ball

DEFENSIVE AREA·

1. Point of distribution?

2. Can we force the ball into an area?
Where?
3. What will be the response of our team
to this?
4. How do we line up our men?
5. What is our response if they still get
the ball out of defence?
6. Do we let them play the early pass?

ATTACKING AREA

1. Is it open play or free hit?
2. Who is marking whom and how?
3. Are we prepared for certain moves?
4. Areas of the circle they prefer to
attack?
5. Do we prefer any one player to have
the ball?

When We Have the Ball

DEFENSIVE AREA

1. Where is our outlet pass?
2. Will they pressurise our defenders?
3. How is our midfield marked?
4. Do we look for long or short passes?
5. Can our defenders come forward with the ball?
6. How do we cope with their midfield marking? Where are the spaces that can be used?

ATTACKING AREA

1. Where are they weakest in relation to our strengths?
2. Are there particular areas that can be exploited?
3. What kind of shots are best?
4. Which set pieces will work best?

General

1. How will the game develop considering the national characteristics, playing record and tournament position of the opposition?
2. How will they try to dominate us?

It is difficult to lay down a formula for producing tactics, but there needs to be a balance between generalisations and attention to detail. This balance will depend upon the time available and the knowledge of the opposition, and although both are always necessary the overriding philosophy must be to prepare team and individual tactics that will enable your pattern of play to dominate for as much of the game as possible, so that you can win. A few particular tactics are given at the end of Chapter 2.

Fig 203   A defender's nightmare! The Australian defender has
been caught flat-footed by the deception of the Pakistan
forward.

10 Training for Hockey

Training should be sensibly organised but it should never be easy.

With apologies to all physiologists reading this chapter, I have kept the theoretical side of the training to a minimum and concentrated upon how these principles can be dovetailed into hockey practices so that physical training and skill practice can develop simultaneously.

TRAINING AREAS

As stated in Chapter 1 the physiological areas that require training or developing are: aerobic stamina; anaerobic stamina; speed; muscular strength; and mobility.

Aerobic Stamina

Aerobic means using oxygen and so this area is concerned with the process of getting oxygen to the working muscles during the game and consists of the lungs, heart, blood vessels and blood. Aerobic training improves the efficiency of this system so that blood laden with oxygen can be distributed more easily to the muscles at any given workload and waste products, such as lactic acid, can be removed more easily. A subsequent result of training is that more work can be done by the player and the recovery rate is improved so that less rest is required between working periods.

For pure aerobic training, running at relatively low speeds for reasonably long distances (6 km) or periods of time (30 minutes) is sufficient, but because the game of hockey is unlike this it may be advantageous to shorten the distance (for example 4 km) and increase the speed. This will introduce an anaerobic aspect into the training, but it will be a beneficial one.

Anaerobic Stamina

Anaerobic means working without oxygen and this occurs when you demand sudden bursts of energy from your body. The aerobic system can keep you working at a low level of output for long periods, but you can only increase the output beyond the capacity of the aerobic system by using the anaerobic system. This system however is split into two parts.

The first is the alactic (or phosphocreatine) energy system and this is able to provide a great deal of energy but is depleted rather rapidly (up to fifteen to twenty seconds of sub-maximal anaerobic activity). However, the replenishment of this energy source is also rapid and it is probable that much of the energy for the bursts of activity in hockey come from this system. Ideally training should be at maximum effort for between five and twenty seconds and with a rest to work ratio of 5:1 with the resting periods being gently active.

The second part of the anaerobic system is the lactic energy system which has the advantage of producing high power output from the muscle for thirty to forty seconds. Unfortunately, the body does not let you have something for nothing and the 'cost' of this output is that lactic acid accumulates in the muscle and has to be cleared by the blood (some is neutralised in the blood while the organs such as the kidneys and liver also help out). At the end of strenuous exercise it is advisable to keep moving so that the blood flow to muscles is maintained in order to clear accumulations of lactic acid (hence the 'warm down'). Training for this system should be done at no less than ninety per cent of maximum effort and the work intervals ought to be between thirty to forty seconds with a rest to work ratio of 3:1. Players should not be asked to do more than six repetitions before a longer rest of eight to ten minutes is given.

Speed and Acceleration

These are self-explanatory and are not the same. Two men may run 100 metres in exactly the same time, but after 20 metres one may be 2 metres ahead of the other. In hockey the ability to accelerate with and run fast with the ball are great assets and while it is possible to improve both speed and acceleration, coaches might be better advised to train players to be able to get as close to their maximum acceleration and running speed while in possession of the ball.

Muscular Strength

This is a great help both for the physical and technical demands of the game. Players should be encouraged to do exercises (using body weight or multi-gym equipment) to improve muscular strength and

endurance in their arms, trunk and legs The actual method of preparing a schedule and the exercises that can be used are widely publicised and if you are in any doubt contact your local Physical Educationalist.

Mobility Exercises

Mobilising is an important aspect of preparing for strenuous activity (match or training session), not only because an improved range of movement in a muscle group may over a period of time help enhance performance but also, and much more important in the short term, it specifically prepares the muscles for the subsequent work by raising their temperature and increasing the blood and oxygen supply.

Exercises for stretching are innumerable but they should cover the major muscle groups and joints (neck, back, hamstrings, gastrocnemius, Achilles tendon, chest, hips, groin, spine, quadriceps, shoulders, abdominals, and so on). These exercises should be done *without* jerking or bobbing.

These activities are usually included in a warm-up before a game or practice session (ten minutes of stretching is the minimum) but other exercises, such as short explosive activities on the major muscle group and performing the skills required in the sport itself, should also be included.

COMBINING TRAINING AND SKILLS

I do not profess to be able to design a training session which produces good physical training effects and good skills practice simultaneously, but I do know from experience that most players train harder physically when skills are included.

Aerobic Training

HOCKEY RUN *(Fig 204)*

This is more interesting than a 4 km run and involves skills. With club players, five continuous circuits followed by a rest or another activity and then five more circuits is demanding.

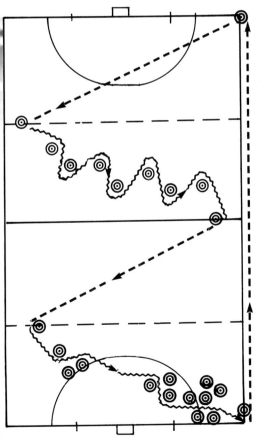

Fig 204

FARTLEK RUNNING

Fartlek, or varied pace, running does not involve skills, but the pace of running can be changed by whoever is leading. Excellent for team spirit!

Anaerobic Training

These activities can be modified to be applicable for either of the anaerobic systems and many of them can be used in sports halls or gymnasiums.

HOCKEY RUN
See Fig 204 above.

Increase pace of running and shorten distance when necessary.

SHUTTLES

Shuttle running between lines varying distances apart.

1. Dribble with ball to each line and back.
2. Dribble to first line and back, run to next line and back, dribble to next line and back and so on. Plus infinite variations!

PAIRS *(Fig 205)*

1. B runs to centre, receives pass, gives it back to A and returns to starting point. Repeat six times or for thirty seconds.
2. A passes to B, who then runs to centre with the ball, returns it to A and runs back to starting point.
3. B runs to centre, receives pass, takes the ball to his starting point and then passes back to A.
4. As in 3, except that as B turns to

149

pass, A runs to the centre, receives the pass, turns and takes the ball back to his starting point, and so on.

Fig 205

FOURS (*Fig 206*)

1. As in *Fig 206*.
2. Vary the types of pass.
3. Vary the angle of pass.
4. Change the position of the balls.
5. Put the central player on the other side.

RELAYS

1. Shuttle relays (*see* above).
2. Passing relays (*see* 'Fours').
3. Dribbling relays over courses with obstacles in varying patterns. These could include slalom courses, random patterns and other exercises to emphasise whatever particular skills the coach wishes to train.

TARGET MAN (*Fig 207*)

1. A, B and C always pass to D. They always pass to the cone towards which D is moving. *Sequence*: A to D, D to C, B to D, D to A, C to D, D to B and so on.

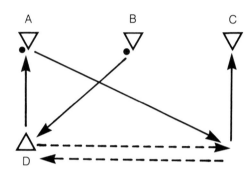

Fig 207

2. The sequence and rules are the same as in 1 but the movement of players is different (*Fig 208*). Every time any player receives a pass he must dribble the ball to a point five metres behind him and then back to his starting point before he passes it.
3. Coaches can make their own further variations.

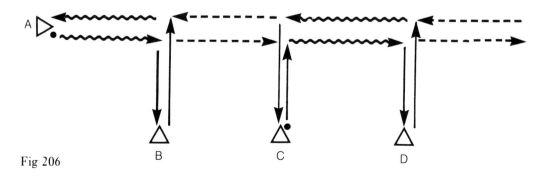

Fig 206

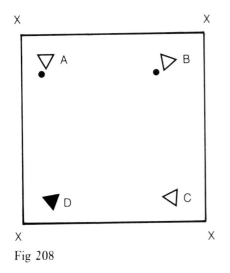

Fig 208

SMALL-SIDED GAMES

Use appropriately sized areas.

1. 3 v 1 possession; keep the ball for thirty seconds.
2. 4 v 2 as in 1 above.
3. 3 v 3 competition to score over a line.
4. 2 v 2 competition to score over a line.
5. 1 v 1 competition to score over a line.

CONCLUSION

Training is concerned with repetition. An international friend of mine once told me that he did all of his training 'in the game'. 'Not possible' I said then and still believe so, but I did find out that he played six games a week!

Training and practising have to be hard but also meaningful, rewarding and fun! I complete this book with a simple but true story. Bernie Cotton, nearing the end of his career, was always followed in alphabetical order in the physical tests by a young man called James Duthie (who incidentally he taught at school!). During a coaching seminar Roger Self was emphasising the character building aspects of early morning hill runs and dwelling on the concept of personal pride. Cotton suggested that it was fine for most, but he had Duthie pounding closely up behind him in spite of the five second interval at the start. 'And how did you feel as he passed you then, Cotton?' asked Self, in his well-known sympathetic voice. 'Very proud of him' replied Bernie.

Index

Assessment
  of players, 143
  of teams, 141–2
Attacking, 85, 91–101

Beating an opponent, 31–41, 57–61, 89–101

Centring, 64–6
Channelling, 75
Closing down, 77
Coach
  communication, 18
  duties, 5
  knowledge, 6, 18
  philosophy, 21
  role, 5
Control
  coaching points, 41
  practices, 47–9
  technique, 41–7
Corners, 119–21
Covering, 74
Creating space, 85–90

Defending
  channelling, 75
  closing down, 77
  covering, 74
  man to man, 104
  marking, 72–4, 104
  objectives of, 103
  positioning, 71
  practices, 73, 77–8
  requirements, 103
  roles, 104–13
  team, 112
  zonal, 104
Dribbling, 33
  coaching points, 35
  practices, 35–41

Fitness, 10
  aerobic, 147
  anaerobic, 147
  mobility, 148

Fitness – *contd.*
  speed and acceleration, 148
  strength, 148
Free hits
  general, 121
  in attack, 125–7
  in defence, 122–4

Goalkeeping
  practices, 138–9
  qualities, 133
  techniques, 133–6
  training, 136–7
Grips, 32–3

Hit-ins, 127–31

Intercepting, 78

Marking, 72
  practices, 73
Methods of play, 6, 21
Motivation, 11

Overlap, 97

Passing
  angled, 49
  flicking, 52
  hitting, 51
  practices, 53–64
  pushing, 51
  square, 49
  through, 49
Penalty corners
  attack, 117–19
  defence, 115–17
Penetrative moves, 89, 91–101
Players
  age and expertise, 12, 17
  assessment, 143
  qualities, 22
  roles, 7, 24–9, 104–13
Principles of attack
  assessment and improvisation, 88

Principles of attack – *contd.*
  mobility, 87
  support, 87
  understanding, 87
  width, 85
Progressive practices
  closing down, 77-8
  control, 47–9
  dribbling, 35–41
  marking, 73
  passing, 53–64
  shooting, 66
  tacking, 82–3
  theory, 13

Restarts from sideline, 127–31

Shooting, 66

Skill learning
  environment, 17
  process, 15
Support play, 69
Systems, 23

Tackling
  coaching points, 78
  forehand, 81
  jab, 79
  reverse stick, 81
  practices, 82–3
Tactics, 8
  at set pieces, 115–31
  in attack, 85, 91–101
  in defence 71–91, 104–13
  planning, 144–5
Team defence, 112

Crowood Sports Books

Badminton – The Skills of the Game	Peter Roper
Basketball – The Skills of the Game	Paul Stimpson
Canoeing – Skills and Techniques	Neil Shave
Coaching Cricket	Keith Andrew
* The Skills of Cricket	Keith Andrew
Fitness for Sport	Rex Hazeldine
* Golf – The Skills of the Game	John Stirling
Hockey – The Skills of the Game	John Cadman
Judo – Skills and Techniques	Tony Reay
Jumping	Malcolm Arnold
Rugby Union – The Skills of the Game	Barrie Corless
Skiing – Developing Your Skill	John Shedden
Sprinting and Hurdling	Peter Warden
Squash – The Skills of the Game	Ian McKenzie
Swimming	John Verrier
Table Tennis – The Skills of the Game	Gordon Steggall
Volleyball – The Skills of the Game	Keith Nicholls

* Also available in paperback

Further details of titles available or in preparation
can be obtained from the publishers.